Nashville Skyline

Bob Dylan's other type of music

Copyright © 2023 Jochen Markhorst
cover design: Jaap de Vries
corrections: Larry Fyffe / Tony Attwood / Stephen Vallely

ISBN: 9798377036241

To Marga

Ev'rything is always right
When I'm alone with you

Contents

The country music station plays soft   7

Thursday, February 13, 1969

1	To Be Alone With You	10
2	I Threw It All Away	33
3	One More Night	39
4	Lay, Lady, Lay	48
5	Western Road	54

Friday, February 14, 1969

6	Peggy Day	65
7	Tell Me That It Isn't True	86
8	Country Pie	91

Monday, February 17, 1969

9	Nashville Skyline Rag	128
10	Tonight I'll Be Staying Here With You	139

Tuesday, February 18, 1969

11	**Girl From The North Country**	**183**
12	**Wanted Man**	**200**

Collateral

13	**Champaign, Illinois**	**228**
14	**Living The Blues**	**242**

It didn't go nowhere   **247**

Sources   **251**

Notes   **253**

"Country music to me doesn't have piano in it, or drums or electric guitars. It must be some other type of music."

- interview with Nick Krewen, *Long Island Voice,* September 11-17, 1997

The country music station plays soft

Four years earlier, Dylan declares in the liner notes to *Bringing It All Back Home*: "I am about t sketch You a picture of what goes on around here sometimes", and he seems to keep that promise, in the next five hundred days, in this mercurial period. Songs, or at least parts of songs on the Holy Trinity *Bringing It All Back Home, Highway 61 Revisited* and *Blonde On Blonde* indeed do suggest impressionism, seem to sketchily express the impressions the young rock poet has to deal with, in this thin wild mercury, tumultuous period of his life.

For the setting of "Visions Of Johanna", for example, the poet seems to sketch a picture of his temporary residence, Room 211 at the Chelsea Hotel. With accompanying soundtrack: *In this room the heat pipes just cough / The country music station plays soft*. At the time, in 1965-66, this may have been difficult to reconcile with the image of the über-cool hipcat Dylan, but by now we have long known that the love for country music is deep and sincere - and that this description of the setting is most likely a truthful *picture of what goes on around here*.

After *Blonde On Blonde*, and after the motorcycle accident (29 July 1966) that marked a long goodbye to the public, Dylan professes his country love anonymously and unheard with his mates from The Band in Woodstock, in the basement of the Big Pink. Without restraint, as we first heard on bootlegs and from 2014 officially on *The Basement Tapes Complete*; Hank Snow, Johnny Cash, Bob Nolan, Hank Williams, Porter Wagoner, Dallas Frazier, Bobby Bare... half the premier league of the Billboard's Hot Country Charts comes along. And just as enthusiastically, Dylan reaches for hardcore, antique country songs like "The Hills Of Mexico" and "Quit Kickin' My Dog Around".

On *John Wesley Harding*, we first hear the love openly, especially in the last two songs ("Down Along The Cove" and "I'll Be Your Baby Tonight") and a little over a year later, when Dylan records *Nashville Skyline* (February 1969), country is embraced completely - in the title, the cover photo, the songs, the arrangements and in the lyrics.

Exactly two years after Dylan recorded "Visions Of Johanna" in Nashville, after Dylan wistfully recalls the soft-playing country music station, the recording of the songs that will fill *Nashville Skyline* begins. And the first song to be recorded on that Thursday, 13th February 1969, 6:00 pm, is probably also the first song that Dylan wrote for this record: "To Be Alone With You".

Thursday, February 13, 1969

6:00-9:00 pm, and 9:00-midnight

Studio A
Columbia Recording Studios
Nashville, Tennessee

Produced by Bob Johnston

Take 1 – 8
To Be Alone With You

Take 9 – 12
I Threw It All Away

Take 13
"Blues"

Take 14 – 19
One More Night

Take 20 – 23
Lay, Lady, Lay.

Take 24
Western Road

Musicians:
Charlie McCoy (bass), Robert S. Wilson (piano and organ), Charlie Daniels (guitar and dobro), Norman L. Blake (guitar), Kenneth Buttrey (drums) and Kelton D. Herston (probably guitar)
9-12: Pete Drake (steel guitar) and Wayne Moss (guitar).

1   To Be Alone With You

I   There was a country radio station, too

Present session musicians Charlie McCoy, Wayne Moss and Kenny Buttrey must have had the pleasant feeling of playing a home game. Dylan's first visit to Nashville, two years ago, had been quite an alienating experience. In many ways. The songs had weird lyrics and were exceptionally long, the musicians were not instructed at all and had to colour the songs as they saw fit, Dylan sat writing for hours in an adjacent room, sessions went on all night... all incomparable with the prevailing hourly-billing mores of recording a ready-made song as quickly as possible to the liking of producer and artist, incomparable with the usual method of working more like a 9-to-5 office job than a rock 'n' roll existence.

But in October '67, for *John Wesley Harding*, at least McCoy (bass) and Buttrey (drums) have already met a different Dylan. Okay, most of the songs are still a bit weird, but almost all have a "normal" length, about three minutes, and the three recording sessions are short and simple, and finished well before midnight. And now, February '69, Dylan is more normal than ever:

"To Be Alone With You" is short (2'10"), has an ordinary chord progression, an ordinary melody and ordinary lyrics; the Nashville Cats are put to work on a song like hundreds they have played and recorded before. And for Dylan, too, it's actually a kind of Trip Down Memory Lane, as we gather from his autobiography:

> "WWOZ was the kind of station I used to listen to late at night growing up, and it brought me back to the trials of my youth and touched the spirit of it. Back then when something was wrong the radio could lay hands on you and you'd be all right. There was a country radio station, too, that came on early, before daylight, that played all the '50s songs, a lot of Western Swing stuff — clip clop rhythms, songs like, "Jingle, Jangle, Jingle," "Under the Double Eagle," "There's a New Moon over My Shoulder," Tex Ritter's "Deck of Cards," which I hadn't heard in about thirty years, Red Foley songs. I listened to that a lot."
>
> (*Chronicles,* Ch. "Oh Mercy")

And now all those hours of listening to the country music station playing soft come out. When Tex Ritter performs his "Deck Of Cards" at the Nashville Club in December '68, he is led in by Canadian Stu Phillips with "How I'd Love To Be Alone With You"; *life's pleasures* from the classic "Hard Times"; *that's the way it oughta be* from Andy Williams' "I Like Your Kind of Love"; Hank Williams echoes in *at the close of the day* ("Help Me Understand") and in *the whole night through* ("Your Cheatin' Heart"), although Dylan might just as well have taken that last one from The Beach Boys' world hit "Wouldn't It Be Nice", of course;

> *Wouldn't it be nice if we could wake up*
> *In the morning when the day is new?*
> *And after having spent the day together*
> *Hold each other close the whole night through*

... and the great happiness from Dylan's last verse, the joy of seeing your loved one after a hard day's night,

> *I'll always thank the Lord*
> *When my working day's through*
> *I get my sweet reward*
> *To be alone with you*

… no doubt reminds Charlie McCoy and Wayne Moss of six years earlier, when they were lucky enough to be on the payroll for the recording of Roy Orbison's masterpiece *In Dreams*, reminds them of "Sunset":

> *At last my working day is done*
> *The setting of the sun has finally come*
> *It's sunset I'm gonna hold my sweetheart*
> *Gonna hold her so tight*

Not to mention the aha-Ray-Charles-moment the entire studio audience must have had at Dylan's bridge: *They say that nighttime is the right time / To be with the one you love.*

In short, the walking jukebox Dylan just shakes out his stetson, this chilly Thursday night in an overcast Nashville. But will take a critical look at the result fifty years later…

II   That boy's good

"Have you written any songs lately for any other artists to do, specifically for that artist? Or any of your old songs," asks Jann Wenner during the *Rolling Stone* interview, November 1969.

> "I wrote To Be Alone With You – that's on Nashville Skyline – I wrote it for Jerry Lee Lewis. [*Laughter*] He was down there when we were listening to the playbacks, and he came in. He was recording an album next door. He listened to it… I think we sent him a dub. Peggy Day – I kind of had the Mills Brothers in mind when I did that one. [*Laughter*]"

Wenner adds *"laughter"* twice, apparently to indicate that both Dylan and his interviewer find the idea of Dylan writing something for Jerry Lee Lewis or something for the Mills Bothers a rather funny joke. Implying, of course, how absurd that would be. However, increased insight suggests that Wenner is either embellishing the written account of the interview with invented atmospheric descriptions after the fact, or that Wenner completely misjudges Dylan's sincerity. The latter is more likely. It is more likely that Wenner is laughing in order to signal that he is sharp enough to recognise that Dylan is throwing a sarcastic side-swipe at Jerry Lee Lewis, and that Dylan is laughing along out of discomfort.

It seems to have escaped Wenner's attention which corner Jerry Lee Lewis is in now, in 1969. The Killer has long since left Sun Records, has taken a different turn and in Nashville is fully immersing himself in pure, hardcore country. The album he records "next door" is the beautiful *She Still Comes Around*, an album filled with honky-tonk and tears-in-your-beer ballads like Merle Haggard's "Today I Started Loving You Again", like "Louisiana Man" and the title track with the brilliant full title "She Still Comes Around (To Love What's Left of Me)", which reaches the second spot on the country singles chart. And will later be played by fan Keith Richards, by the way, on a curious 1977 bootleg on which Keef accompanies himself surprisingly skilfully on piano.

The Killer's love of country is as deep and intrinsic as Dylan's. Before this record, Jerry Lee had already scored with his comeback album *Another Place, Another Time*, which earned him two Top 5 singles and even won the heart of country god George Jones. And after *She Still Comes Around*, the one he records while Dylan is recording *Nashville Skyline* next door, Jerry Lee stays in Nashville, for the time being. Still in this same year of 1969, he will release *Sings the Country Music Hall of Fame Hits, Vol. 1* and *Sings the Country Music Hall of Fame Hits, Vol. 2*, albums that totally live up to their titles. "Oh, Lonesome Me", "I'm So Lonesome I Could Cry", "I Wonder Where You Are Tonight", "Jackson", "Cold, Cold Heart", "He'll Have To Go"... they're all on there, the landmarks of country, the songs that, one way or another, have all trickled into Dylan's oeuvre.

In short, it is not at all absurd or laughable to go along with Dylan's idea that "To Be Alone With You" would fit perfectly on the album The Killer is recording next door. But alas, apparently Lewis is not impressed. Or, more likely, he thinks the song's content doesn't fit in among all those tearjerkers on *She Still Comes Around* - after all, Dylan's lyrics are rather cute and cloudless. Incidentally, Dylan's anecdote seems to be contradicted by the stories surrounding "Rita May", the first Dylan song Jerry Lee will record.

Ten years later, in 1979, The Killer enthusiastically returns to his rockabilly roots for another comeback album (*Jerry Lee Lewis*, with the hit "Rockin' My Life Away"). Producer Bones Howe has Dylan under his skin. Apart from being from Minnesota too, Howe's impressive career (Elvis, Mamas & Papas, Tom Waits) started with Dylan; his breakthrough as a producer is the 1965 hit he produced for The Turtles, Dylan's "It Ain't Me, Babe". So, obviously, Bones has warm feelings for Bob Dylan. For Jerry Lee's comeback, he proposes a bare-bones band (including Elvis' guitarist James Burton), and takes care of a strong tracklist. Charlie Rich's "Who Will The Next Fool Be", for example, and Arthur Alexander's "Every Day I Have To Cry". And he nominates Dylan's throwaway "Rita May" already at the first recording session, "a simple fifties rock thing" according to co-author Jacques Levy.

The song is a product of Dylan's collaboration with Levy, the experiment that would lead to the world successes "Hurricane" and *Desire* (1976). Lewis slams "Rita May" on the tape with gusto and full commitment, and it's only when he's listening back that he remembers to ask producer Howe: "Say, who wrote this?" "Bob Dylan," Howe replies, grinning, for he is sure that Lewis will be mighty surprised. But The Killer doesn't seem to recognise the name at all. *"That boy's good,"* Jerry Lee Lewis says, "I'll do anything by him."

This is January 1979, a little less than ten years after Jerry Lee, according to Dylan, has been listening to playbacks of "To Be Alone With You" with him, in the control room of Columbia Studio in Nashville. It doesn't seem very likely that Dylan would make this up, in the interview with Wenner conducted eight months after that alleged meeting. More likely, The Killer has already forgotten that February 1969 interlude ten years later. Or, even more likely, that the name *"Dylan"* meant as little to him then as it does today, in January 1979. Anyway, Lewis' highly quotable *"I'll do anything by him"* is therefore pertinently incorrect - he was handed "To Be Alone With You" on a silver platter at the time, but he left the song uncommented upon the studio floor.

Much later again, 35 years after that first Dylan cover to be precise, yet another skilful producer with Dylan roots takes care of yet another Jerry Lee Lewis comeback album. In 2014, Daniel Lanois produces *Rock & Roll Time*, a kind of return to the 1950s, to Sun Records. Like his predecessor Bones Howe, Lanois cleans out the studio and restricts himself to a basic rock 'n' roll band to accompany Jerry Lee (featuring Dylan drummer Jim Keltner), and like his predecessor Bones Howe, Lanois also nominates a Dylan throwaway from the 70s, which - history repeats itself - is picked up enthusiastically and wholeheartedly: Jerry Lewis Lee's cover of Dylan's "Stepchild" is exciting, heavy and swampy. And underlines once again that The Killer should have accepted Dylan's "To Be Alone With You". *That boy is really good.*

III   Shadow Kingdom

"His playing would rip your head off," says John Fogerty in his autobiography, very Dylanesque, about bluegrass legend Earl Scruggs. Fogerty, like Dylan in *Chronicles*, has in his own memoir *Fortunate Son* (2015) a sympathetic tendency of swooning, in often poetic, though sometimes alienating superlatives over musicians he admires. With great overlap, by the way. Hank Williams (*"Your Cheatin' Heart* just slayed me"), Link Wray, Charley Patton, Buck Owens, Merle Haggard... well, Fogerty, of course, has also exhaustively demonstrated his deep-rooted love of country and bluegrass (most notably on his solo debut, the 1973 country tribute record *The Blue Ridge Rangers*).

Anyway, Earl Scruggs. Dylan's awe is visible, in the documentary shot in 1970, *Earl Scruggs - His Family and Friends*. The soundtrack of the same name (released 2005) features five Dylan songs. Three that Earl performs with Joan Baez ("Love Is Just A Four Letter Word", "It Ain't Me, Babe" with Baez's witty Dylan imitation, and "I Dreamed I Saw St. Augustine"), one with The Byrds ("You Ain't Goin' Nowhere", of course) and one with Dylan himself: "Nashville Skyline Rag". In the documentary, we see another song played by the two legends together (the age-old classic "East Virginia Blues"), but not the two songs played by Scruggs, his sons Randy and Gary, and Dylan: "Honey, Just Allow Me One More Chance" and... "To Be Alone With You". The mono recordings of these are finally heard on disc 3 of *The Bootleg Series 15 - Travelin' Thru, 1967-1969* (2019).

The session takes place on 17 May 1970, half a year after the *Rolling Stone* interview in which Dylan dreams about Jerry Lee Lewis adding the song to his repertoire. Apparently, Dylan has given up hope, and now suspects that he can do Earl Scruggs a favour with it. But he is not an inspired salesman. We hear Dylan's hesitant beginning, he seems to be looking for the melody, then he starts in the middle of the song, on the second line of the second verse ("*At the close of day*"), sings that second verse twice, and the rest of the song is not very steady either - he changes lines, forgets words and makes up other, hardly impressive words on the spot. It is, all in all, justifiable that documentary maker David Hoffman left this fragment on the cutting floor.

For the time being, it is the last time Dylan will concern himself with "To Be Alone With You". The song disappears into a drawer and is only retrieved twenty years later: its live debut is 15 October 1989 in Pennsylvania. As an opener even. Dylan seems to be in a conservative country mood these days. "Man In The Long Black Coat" is also performed for the first time this week, the setlist includes songs like the Civil War ballad "Two Soldiers", "Precious Memories", "Lakes Of Pontchartrain" and "Barbara Allen"... but "To Be Alone With You" has become a solid, energetic Jerry Lee Lewis-like rocker.

And he seems pleased with it. The song remains on the set list, always as the opener, and is also taken to Europe the following year; Dylan opens his concerts in Paris and London with "To Be Alone With You" as well. The song becomes a mainstay of the Never Ending Tour; apart from 1997 it is on the setlist every year, and, until its temporary retirement in 2005, is eventually performed 123 times.

This time the song seems to have been discarded for good. In the fourteen years from 2006 until the covid emergency stop in 2019, Dylan performs more than 1200 times, and "To Be Alone With You" remains in the drawer. But then it's 2021, Dylan rejoices fans with the online "concert" *Shadow Kingdom* and surprises them with wonderful interpretations, beautiful performances and, above all, the resurrection of a fully restored "To Be Alone With You".

The rock 'n' roll is gone. Actually, so is the country. The accordion gives the song a Tex-Mex flavour, Dylan's recitation tends towards vaudeville, the band towards pop, but above all: almost every line of the lyrics has been changed.

Lyric changes in themselves are not too remarkable with Dylan, but such a radical and complete text revision is - we only know it from a handful of songs from the bard's immense oeuvre. "Down Along The Cove", "Gonna Change My Way of Thinking", a few songs of which he later (largely) returns to the original lyrics ("Tangled Up In Blue", "Simple Twist Of Fate")... there are not many more.

Dylan is asked a few times about these frequent and sometimes radical changes of lyrics. In the fascinating interview for *SongTalk* (with Paul Zollo, April '91) he kind of shrugs his shoulders an says:

> "They're songs. They're not written in stone. They're on plastic. Somebody told me that Tennyson often wanted to rewrite his poems once he saw them in print."

... and similar vagueness ("The original lyrics weren't fair to me because they just didn't feel right at the time," regarding "Tangled Up In Blue"). Fascinating it is nevertheless - if only because it offers a glimpse into the creative mind of a Nobel Prize-winning poet.

The original first verse, like the rest of the lyrics, is not too titanic - *written on plastic*, indeed:

> *To be alone with you*
> *Just you and me*
> *Now won't you tell me true*
> *Ain't that the way it oughta be?*
> *To hold each other tight*
> *The whole night through*
> *Ev'rything is always right*
> *When I'm alone with you*

Okay, the rhyme scheme (*ABAB-CACA*) is quite unusual, but the content is a saltless accumulation of clichés. Maybe that's what triggers Dylan to change it fifty years later to:

> *To be alone with you, just you and I*
> *Under the moon, 'neath the star-spangled sky*
> *I know you're alive, and I am too*
> *My one desire is to be alone with you*

Which is a bit puzzling. At first glance, the changes are hardly spectacular. In *Lyrics* and other official publications, the stanzas are indeed formatted as eight-line stanzas, but during the rewriting session Dylan apparently structured it the way he sings it: four lines, quatrains, and the simplest rhyme scheme (*AABB*). Perhaps the poet has indeed searched for a Verlaine-like mosaic of rhyme and assonance; *you* in line 1 assonant with *moon* in line 2; *sky* in line 2 with *I* in line 3; *alive* in line 3 with *desire* in line 4... too consistent to be coincidental, in any case. However, this melodious artifice is abandoned right from verse two - the poet has either already grown tired of it, or this steady pattern of assonances indeed was accidental after all.

In terms of content, again at first glance, there doesn't seem to be much going on either; at most, one wonders why Dylan took the trouble to replace one cliché with another. *Under the moon, my one desire, the star spangled sky...* all as clichéd as *the whole night through* and *hold each other tight*. But then there is that one line, that one splinter that makes the listener look up: "I know you're alive, and I am too". A line that would rip your head off.

IV   Beware of his promise

Frankie Valli likes to act and does it quite well. Mostly mafioso types (*Miami Vice, Witness To The Mob, The Sopranos*), but his music career always comes first. "They made all the changes for me and rescheduled shooting because they knew I was on tour a lot," he says in the interview with *SongFacts* (July 2014), "... and I knew I had to be killed off. Either that or I'd have to quit my touring business." That role in *The Sopranos* (as Rusty Millio, "The Mayor of Munchkinville") is memorable and provides yet another boost to Valli's already impressive, nearly sixty-year career.

When the interviewer asks him about the secret behind the success of that endless string of hits (Valli has scored 39 Billboard Top 40 hits with and without the Four Seasons, seven of them No. 1 and eleven Top 10 hits), Valli has a simple and rather Dylanesque explanation: you got to change, you got to go to new places. And *great songs*. "You need to have great songs. It always boils down to the same thing."

That is indeed a special talent of Valli and his comrades: recognising a great song. "Can't Take My Eyes Off Of You", "December, 1963", "Beggin'", "Working My Way Back To You"... great songs, evergreens by now, whose potential was first recognised by The Four Seasons. It doesn't always work out, Valli tells us. Their recording of Boz Scaggs' "We're All Alone", for example, was rejected by the record company and six months later

Rita Coolidge scored her worldwide hit with it. And Valli himself was very fond of "The Night", which was not promoted, did not become a hit, but - through mysterious ways - somehow reached the Top 10 in the UK three years later.

Part of that song's success is undoubtedly due to its *northern soul* vibe, and to the trend of English DJs seeking to popularise forgotten and overlooked records. Sometimes with overwhelming success; "Tainted Love" is an obscure B-side to a totally flopped single from 1965 ("My Bad Boy's Comin' Home", by Gloria Jones), and is after its success in the English clubs in '76 recorded again by the enchanting Gloria (produced by her life partner Marc Bolan, by the way). Again failing to chart, but noticed by the wardrobe boy, Marc Almond, the colourful bird of paradise who elevates the song to a world hit in 1981 with his Soft Cell. Almond too, at least twice, has that enviable talent for unleashing hidden hit potential. In Soft Cell's repertoire, "Tainted Love" replaces Almond's initial first choice, "The Night" (which Soft Cell still will record in 2003) - which, incidentally, would probably have been a hit as well, if it hadn't been for "Tainted Love".

The appeal of both "Tainted Love" and "The Night" to Almond can be felt. It is the same appeal that Dylan feels and, especially in the twenty-first century, displays in songs like "Scarlet Town", "Make You Feel My Love" and "Soon After Midnight": songs that only reveal a sinister, dark undercurrent on second listen. Which sometimes remains entirely under the surface, even. "Make You Feel My Love", in particular, is generally understood to be a tender declaration of love, but on second listen really does seem more like a threatening letter from a persistent stalker. "The Night" is even more oppressive;

> *Beware of his promise*
> *Believe what I say*
> *Before the night is ending*
> *Be sure of what you're saying*

... words of a seemingly benevolent comrade, who warns a naïve lass about the imposter who has taken her in. Strangely enough, however, the first person narrator then lists a whole series of actions that are actually only sweet and nice;

> *Cause he paints a pretty picture*
> *And he tells you that he needs you*
> *And he covers you with roses*
> *And he always keeps you dreaming*

... and it goes on like this. Actions of an infatuated, well-meaning lover, in any case. What the lady should be wary of is completely unclear. Even more eyebrow-raising is the "warning" four lines later:

> *If he always keeps you dreaming*
> *You won't have a lonely hour*
> *If the day could last forever*
> *You might like your ivory tower*

"*You might like your ivory tower*"? That is the same, anomalous use of the term "ivory tower" as in Dylan's revised "To Be Alone With You" from 2021:

> *To be alone with you, even for just an hour*
> *In a castle high, in an ivory tower*
> *Some people don't get it, they just don't have a clue*
> *They wouldn't know what it's like to be alone with you*

... an ivory tower as an image of an idyllic, romantic love nest. Without the usual negative connotations of "lack of concern", "unaware of wordly affairs", "isolated". The connotations, in any case, as we know them from dozens of songs. From Porter Wagoner's "Ivory Tower", for instance (*Don't lock yourself in your ivory tower don't keep our souls far apart*), from Wanda Jackson's "Fallin'" (*I thought that love could never touch me / And then my ivory tower toppled*) and from the most beautiful of all, Van Morrison's "Ivory Tower" from 1986:

> *When you come down from your Ivory Tower*
> *You will see how it really must be*
> *When you come down from your Ivory Tower*
> *You will see how it really must be*
> *To be like me, to see like me*
> *To feel like me*

... a lyric with a strong "Positively 4th Street" vibe, as it were. But then again: Dylan rewrites his "To Be Alone With You" into a brooding, murderous thriller – a sinister protagonist who wants to lure his victim to a *castle high* with an *ivory tower* does contribute to the gothic, nineteenth-century shadowy kingdom-setting that Dylan is so fond of, in his late work.

V The Big Sleep

As with the text changes of the first verse, the rewritten bridge also seems unspectacular at first glance. In 1969, Dylan wrote and sang:

> *They say that nighttime is the right time*
> *To be with the one you love*
> *Too many thoughts get in the way in the day*
> *But you're always what I'm thinkin' of*

 ... so clichéd and clumsy as to be almost comical. "Nighttime is the right time to be with the one you love" is a lazy copy/paste from the song the whole world has been singing along for years now with Nappy Brown (1957) or with Ray Charles (1958), or with Rufus and Carla (1964). A song that is actually much older, by the way; already in 1937 Roosevelt Sykes recorded "Night Time Is the Right Time"... with exactly these very same words.

Not to mention the dull "in the way in the day" and the weak closing line. Which, to make it even more awkward, is a semantically incorrect continuation of the previous one - if I *always* think of you, there won't be, obviously, "too many thoughts in the way". Not during the day either.

Irrelevant, of course - the Nobel Prize winner is not aiming here for a gripping epic about a scorching love, nor for a heartbreaking lyrical declaration of love, but is quite content with an accumulation of empty clichés. "Words don't interfere," as he would later explain (*Playboy* interview with Ron Rosenbaum, 1978). Anyway, fifty years later, the poet revises the bridge;

> *They say the nighttime is the right time to hold each other tight*
> *All worldly cares will disappear and everything will come outright*

... starting off again with a puzzling intervention; one cliché is exchanged for another ("to hold each other tight"), which seems rather pointless. Well, perhaps Dylan changed it because he finds the uncritical copying of the second part ("to be with the one you love") a bit too easy-going or corny by now.

The second line, then, is a real enrichment. The disappearing *worldly cares* in the bridge also builds a substantive bridge to the preceding *ivory tower* and *high castle*, the crime scene to which the narrator wants to take his victim. An ivory tower, after all, is a synonym for detachment, an absence of worldly concerns. And, remarkably enough, *worldly cares* is a relatively uncommon word combination in the art of song. The old Rodgers/Hart jazz standard "Blue Room" comes to mind, there are not many more examples. In which, by the way, the *blue room* is also something like an ivory tower, a place where the protagonist and his beloved can isolate themselves from everyday worries. *Really* isolate themselves - - even Robinson Crusoe is still closer to bleak reality;

> *You sew your trousseau,*
> *and Robinson Crusoe,*
> *Is not so far from worldly cares,*
> *As our blue room, far away upstairs*

Dylan presumably knows Bing Crosby's rendition (1956), or Perry Como's hit (1948), and the cinephile Dylan will have noticed the song on the soundtrack of *The Big Sleep* as well; from that film, Dylan also records "You Go To My Head" and "I'll Guess I'll Have To Change My Plans" (both on *Triplicate*, 2017), and "And Her Tears Flowed Like Wine" is played by the DJ in his *Theme Time Radio Hour* (episode 39, "Tears")... every song from *The Big Sleep* comes along with Dylan sooner or later. Apart from that, he undoubtedly considered "Blue Room" in his American Songbook years 2015-2017.

Still, it is probably only an unconscious echo, this *worldly cares*, or perhaps just a coincidence - but in any case it flows smoothly and pleasantly into the continuation, into the half Gandhi quote ("Therefore, replace greed by love and everything will come outright"); on both a substantive and an instinctive level, a successful match with *disappearing worldly cares*. Gandhi is anything but a high castle dweller in an ivory tower, but he is, of course, detachment incarnate.

And a more macabre interpretation of this seemingly lovely bridge is offered in hindsight, when we hear whereto the bridge is being laid:

> *I wish the night was here, make me scream and shout*
> *I'll fall into your arms, I'll let it all hang out*
> *I'll hound you to death, that's just what I'll do*
> *I won't sleep a wink 'till I'm alone with you*

... the verse that marks a definitive break with the tenor of the original text. The first six words remain unchanged, but after that, the tide turns quite drastically;

> *I wish the night were here*
> *Bringin' me all of your charms*
> *When only you are near*
> *To hold me in your arms*
> *I'll always thank the Lord*
> *When my working day's through*
> *I get my sweet reward*
> *To be alone with you*

... the closing couplet of the original version. Not-a-care-in-the-world words as they have echoed against the walls of Nashville studios for decades, words we have all heard dozens of times in songs by Hank Snow and Roy Orbison, by Hank Williams and Glen Campbell. But there is little left of these innocent words. The safe and obedient "I'll always thank the Lord" is rewritten as "I'll hound you to death", the sweet and cute "all of your charms" is now "scream and shout"... the hard-working, God-fearing sweetheart from 1969 is transformed into a bloodthirsty sexual predator who will not rest until he has that girl in his claws, until he is alone with her. Upon which he shall put her to a Big Sleep, we may fear.

VI Penthouse Serenade

Max Fleischer left quite a lot to be grateful for, and in the Top 3 of Fleischer's gratifying creations is Betty Boop. Certainly, the twentieth century would have been a duller one without the frenzied 1930s masterpieces featuring the archetypal Jazz Age flapper Betty Boop. Like *Minnie The Moocher* (1932) and especially *Snow-White* (1933), the brilliant, swinging fantasies fluttering around Cab Calloway's "Minnie The Moocher" and Cab's irresistible rendition of "St. James Infirmary Blues" (Dylan's template for "Blind Willie McTell"). Featuring Koko The Clown as vocalist, in flawless Calloway choreography.

Fleischer, like Frankie Valli, has a nose for great songs and sees their added value for his cartoons. At least as irresistible as the use of Cab Calloway's songs and stage presence are guest roles for stars such as Rudy Vallée (*Kitty from Kansas City*), Maurice Chevalier (*Stopping the Show*) and Louis Armstrong (*I'll Be Glad When You're Dead You Rascal You*). And the songs Betty sings herself, of course.

Three weeks before Fleischer surprises with *Snow-White* in March 1933, he produces the beautiful 6-minutes interlude *Betty Boop's Penthouse*, for which he mines the then relatively unknown "Penthouse Serenade (When We're Alone)". Fleischer has probably heard the version by Roy Fox & his Band, or the primal version by Tom Gerun and His Orchestra, but thanks to Betty Boop, the song makes its way to the general public, and later, via Nat King Cole, Anita O'Day and Tony Bennett, to the American Songbook - from which a Marianne Faithfull, for instance, digs it up again (*Strange Weather*, 1987).

It has a nice, classic melody, and the beautiful lyrics with nice, Cole Porter-like rhymes are thematically in themselves a fairly common Depression-era aspiration from a penniless, love-struck protagonist who dreams of the glamour of an uptown Manhattan flat;

> *Just picture a penthouse way up in the sky*
> *With hinges on chimneys for stars to go by*
> *A sweet slice of Heaven for just you and I*
> *When we're alone.*
>
> *From all of society we'll stay aloof*
> *And live in propriety there on the roof.*
> *Two heavenly hermits we will be in truth*
> *When we're alone.*
>
> *We'll see life's mad patterns*
> *As we view old Manhattan*
> *Then we can thank our lucky stars*
> *That we're living as we are.*

A protagonist who wants to take the woman of his dreams to *a castle high*, to his *ivory tower*, where they will be alone... *to be alone with you*, in short. Not necessarily very original, but the use of the atypical *mad patterns* (wildly rhyming with *Manhattan*) in the bridge suggests where Dylan at least got the inspiration for his text revision of "To Be Alone With You".

On *Nashville Skyline*, in 1969, "To Be Alone With You" isn't very long: 2'06". Shorter, actually; the first twelve seconds the band fiddle around, Dylan asks producer Johnston "Is it rolling Bob?", and he doesn't start singing until after 12 seconds. Fifty years later, in the *Shadow Kingdom*, the song clocks in at 2'58". Dylan starts singing at 1 second, the tempo is slightly faster, and Dylan sings his last notes, a repeat of the last line, at 2'41". The last seventeen seconds are a short instrumental coda. All in all, more than 50% longer than the original. Which can be explained quite simply: the rewritten version has a bridge and a verse more. In 1969 Dylan sings 157 words, in 2021 it's 208.

The extra verse is introduced with that new bridge:

I'm collecting my thoughts in a pattern, moving from place to place
Stepping out into the dark night, stepping out into space

... in which Dylan's words, of course, take on a completely different connotation than those in "Penthouse Serenade". "*Thoughts in a pattern*", "*stepping out*", "*into the dark*", "*into space*"... all metaphors that could signal a mental disorder, suggesting that a protagonist here is expressing his descent into madness. Which is confirmed in the following closing couplet:

What happened to me, darling? What was it you saw?
Did I kill somebody? Did I escape the law?
Got my heart in my mouth, my eyes are still blue
My mortal bliss is to be alone with you

Lurid words. The series of questions insinuates that the first-person narrator lost his self-control and in a frenzy, or at least in a different state of consciousness, committed bloody mischief. What is even more disturbing is the apparently reassuring meant observation *"my eyes are still blue"*. The narrator can only reassure himself with this fact by standing in front of a mirror - which would imply that he has posed the previous questions to himself, to his own reflection. Which in turn suggests a Dr Jeckyll/Mr Hyde type of schizophrenia, or rather, given the choice of words, a Gollum/Sméagol-like psychopathological discord;

> Gollum: What's it saying, my precious, my love? Is Sméagol losing his nerve?
> Sméagol: No! Not! Never! Sméagol hates nasty hobbitses! Sméagol wants to see them... dead!
> Gollum: Patience! Patience, my love. First we must lead them to her.

The blue-eyed protagonist standing in front of the mirror gets no answer, and it is to be feared that he asks his questions over the still warm corpse of his guest, of the lady lured to his castle high, his ivory tower, his penthouse way up in the sky. Which doesn't seem to bother him too much: *"My mortal bliss is to be alone with you."*

Antique-sounding words, which Dylan has used once before, in a similar sultry, oppressive context:

> *My wretched heart's pounding*
> *I felt an angel's kiss*
> *My memories are drowning*
> *In mortal bliss*

... in "Beyond The Horizon" (2006). Where those words are introduced with *"Beyond the horizon someone prayed for your soul"* and concluded with *"Every step that you take, I'm walking the same"*; with similar creepy, sinister words.

The antique-like colour of the final words is explainable, by the way. On *Modern Times*, the 2006 album on which "Beyond The Horizon" can be found, Dylan embellishes more lyrics with lovingly stolen Ovid fragments. The text of "Beyond The Horizon" as it appears in the official publications, in *Lyrics 1961-2012* and on the official site, is for unknown reasons completely different from the text Dylan sings on the album, and the above bridge is not found there - but Dylan does sing it. Including the words lovingly stolen from Ovid: *"my wretched heart"* (found in both *Tristia* and *Metamorphoses*) and the *"mortal bliss"*, from "Minos" in *Metamorphoses Book 7*, where it is usually translated as:

> *But mortal Bliss will never come sincere,*
> *Pleasure may lead, but Grief brings up the Rear*

... yep, with yet again subcutaneous menace. An inescapable darkness with which even Betty Boop's version of "Penthouse Serenade" closes:

> *In my little penthouse I'll always contrive*
> *To keep love and romance forever alive*
> *In view of the Hudson just over the drive,*
> *For I'm alone.*

2   I Threw It All Away

"There was always something about that song, that was so simple, and an audacity to this sort of simplicity to that song. But it was so... so powerful at the same time. For me, at least. I was always ragingly envious of that song."

... said Nick Cave when asked if there is a song that he wished he had written himself. A fan could have guessed that Cave would pick "I Threw It All Away". For over twenty years, the story has been going around that he buys a copy of Dylan's *Nashville Skyline* in every city he visits, and the source of that story is Cave himself, in an interview with Andy Gill for Q magazine, May '95:

"I constantly buy the same record over and over again: I've bought so many versions of *Nashville Skyline* – I must be keeping Dylan in... whatever that is he needs keeping in."

And when the Australian is asked in 1997 to provide the music for the film *To Have And To Hold*, an Original Soundtrack is recorded with twenty original compositions and one cover: "I Threw It All Away", sung by the legendary Scott Walker.

The former singer of the gothic punk band The Birthday Party, who releases high-quality solo albums almost every year from the 1980s, is a seasoned Dylan fan. In his compilation "The Sick Bag Song", a collection of thoughts, poems and sketches that he notes on the puke bags during his many flying hours, we also find the poetic representation of the first and only encounter with his hero (Glastonbury, 1998):

> Then slowly, extending from his sleeve,
> A cold, white, satin hand took mine.
> *Hey, I like what you do*, he said to me.
> *I like what you do, too*, I replied. I nearly died.
> Then his hand retracted up his sleeve,
> And Bob Dylan turned and took his leave,
> Disappearing back into the rain.

In an interview, he confesses to have been completely starstruck, although he retells it, here too, in a romanticised way:

> "It was raining heavily and I was standing in the doorway of my trailer in the band enclosure, watching the water rise quicker and quicker, so that now it was running into my trailer. There was a crack of thunder, I looked up and saw a man in a hooded windcheater rowing a tiny boat across the enclosure toward me. The water is now up to my knees. The man pulls the boat in and extends a hand that has a long thumbnail. His hand in mine feels smooth and cold, but giving. The man, who is Bob Dylan, says something like, "I like your stuff," and before I can reply, he turns the boat around and rows back to his trailer."

Heart-warming little anecdote, although the decor, as we can see in the photo, is slightly less apocalyptic. But Dylan's approval of Cave's work is credible. Probably the bard is very charmed by his album *Murder Ballads* (1996), which contains idiosyncratic versions of "Stagger Lee" and "Henry Lee", two age-old folk songs that are also on Dylan's pedestal, as well as a dark, foreboding interpretation of Dylan's own "Death Is Not The End". The other seven songs, including the world hit "Where The Wild Roses Grow", all tell macabre, sinister murders and massacres.

Obviously, the admired "I Threw It All Away" is far from lurid or bloody, but apart from that "audacious simplicity", the sombre load will have touched Cave. Yet the seismic shock that *Nashville Skyline* causes when released is not due to these characteristics, but mainly to Dylan's voice, a crooning, smooth country tenor, to the country content of the music and to the enormous contrast with his previous albums. In Dylan's catalog, those three labels are still intact, but the dismay among the fans has gradually evaporated. The crown jewel of the album, "Lay Lady Lay", continues to score high in favourites lists and hit charts. Album finale "Tonight I'll Be Staying Here With You" penetrates thanks to adaptations by top artists such as Johnny Cash, Jeff Beck and Ben E. King the canon. And also "I Threw It All Away" does have some pretty heavy advocates; apart from Nick Cave also a Mr. Costello and a George Harrison, MBE, for example.

In itself the song is lyrically little uplifting. It is, within the country tradition, a ten-a-penny jeremiad of a pining narrator, who bitterly blames himself for losing the love of his life through his own misconduct. Theme and choice of words are not essentially different from half the repertoire of Dylan's old heroes Hank Williams or George Jones. One scrap of Dylan's poetic brio flashes in the lines *Once I had mountains in the palm of my hand / And rivers that ran through ev'ry day*, but the contrast with the lyrics of songs like "Visions Of Johanna" and "All Along The Watchtower" is overwhelming - and that contrast, this *Flowers In The Dirt* effect, unintentionally adds to the appeal. In addition to that *audacious simplicity*, the mental change catches the eye, obviously; no poisonous reproaches, no kick after she's down, but a broken, humble first person who searches his own conscience - it definitely is a new Dylan.

The strongest pillar, however, is the music. The chord scheme plays an attractive game with the listener's expectations, threatening to drive the melody into a ditch a few times. After the conventional accompaniment under the first two lines, Dylan the Musician suddenly takes a turn to a major chord at *But I was cruel* (where one would expect minor) and then takes a completely unusual detour back to the starting point, as Tony Attwood clearly demonstrates on his blog *Untold Dylan,* December 6, 2015:

> "What makes the song be so adaptable to different re-workings is that the opening forces us to give full attention on the melody, as the chords are running through the everyday C, Am, F, C routine (a chord sequence almost as common as the 12 bar blues).
>
> But when faced with the line "But I was cruel" Dylan reflects the sudden change in the story line by jerking us totally and unexpectedly into the chord of A major, and from there to D minor. Whether you know anything about music or not, there is every chance you will find what is happening in the music a bit like being pushed over… you are toppling backwards not knowing where you are going.
>
> And even after that you still don't know because although the guitar comes back to C, the key chord, it then adds in E minor straight after, which we haven't heard before, before solidifying in the world we came from.
>
> In other words, we think we know where we are, but suddenly the words, the chords and the melody conspire to jerk us out of our complacency. It is a very hard trick to pull without it sounding horribly false, but Dylan does it superbly, which is why the song works."
>
> (Tony Attwood, "Bob Dylan, after the crash", *Untold Dylan*)

A weird route, almost a guarantee for false slips in the melody, but Dylan does the job seemingly effortlessly.

In the bridge the master plays a comparable trick, in the deceptive *Love is all there is*. Deceptive, because the middle-eight would have been intolerably sweet in an obvious blues scheme. This musical setting, though, provides the welcome angularity.

Plenty of covers, of course - after all, it *is* a beautiful Dylan song. Elvis Costello's version is a highlight of his cover album *Kojak Variety* (1995). Madeleine Peyroux produces beautiful, jazzy interpretations of Dylan's work and her "I Threw It All Away" on *Standing On The Rooftop* is also a direct hit (2011, which incidentally also contains a chilling "Love In Vain", from Robert Johnson). And usual suspect Jimmy LaFave has both the blues and the country in his genes, and proves that on *Trail* (1999).

However, the most beautiful covers are injected with soul. One of the finest in that category comes from The Bo-Keys, a reunion-like band from Memphis that has the laudable ambition to restore the legendary Memphis sound for the 21st century. That works contagiously well, as with the cover of "I Threw It All Away" on *Heartaches By The Number* (2016).

The most irresistible is a lot older. Cher has culpable Dylan fiascos on her conscience, but in 1969 everything is right. The Californian with Armenian roots is indeed one of the most successful artists in pop history - she is the only artist to score a number 1 hit in six (!) consecutive decades - but in the late 1960s her career experienced a first dip. For the restart, she hires the famous producer Jerry Wexler and submits to his regime at the legendary Muscle Shoals Sound Studio in Alabama. The same producer and the same studio (and the same co-producer Barry Beckett on the keys) who will help Dylan ten years later with his best-sounding album *Slow Train Coming*.

Chers *3614 Jackson Highway* is also a minor masterpiece, but unfortunately commercially a flop. Eleven excellent covers, sparkling, soulfully arranged and an outstandingly singing Cher. Wexler is a big Dylan fan and so is Cher, so it's no surprise that three of the eleven songs are from the Great White Wonder. Surprising still is that all three songs have been picked from the recent *Nashville Skyline* (also "Lay Lady Lay" and "Tonight I'll Be Staying Here With You") and even more astounding is the compelling impulse that the already so melancholic original gets from Beckett's piano and from the Muscle Shoals Horns, the wind section.

At best a Dusty Springfield had surpassed it, presumably.

3   One More Night

I   There's A Tear In My Beer

Arguably one of the prettiest, though one of the most middle-of-the-road songs on *Nashville Skyline* is "One More Night". And arguably the song with the most remarkable vocals, too. Even among all those other songs sung with that remarkable new, smoothly crooning voice. "Everybody remarks on the change of your singing style," says *Rolling Stone* editor Jann Wenner in the inter-view, June 1969.

> "Well, Jann, I'll tell you something. There's not too much of a change in my singing style, but I'll tell you something which is true... I stopped smoking. When I stopped smoking my voice changed... So drastically, I couldn't believe it myself. That's true. I tell you, you stop smoking those cigarettes [*laughter*]... and you'll be able to sing like Caruso."

Which, of course, is total bullshit. Dylan is in Nashville, recording a country album with country musicians, has written country songs and is looking for a country voice. Hank Williams' quiver and yodel soon sound too artificial, tenor Caruso's high D and depth are obviously a bridge too far, but in the vast prairie between those two extremes are plenty of light, velvety baritone voices that Dylan can come close to. Hank Snow, in particular - a country hero who has been under his skin since puberty anyway.

"I'd always listened to Hank Snow," Dylan says to Sam Shepard *(True Dylan*, 1986), and it's demonstrably true. In the Basement, the men play "I Don't Hurt Anymore"; on *Down In The Groove*, Dylan covers "Ninety Miles An Hour"; in the 1970s, he records "A Fool Such As I"; in 1985, he names Snow's "Lady's Man" first in a list of "a dozen influential records"; and as a DJ in the twenty-first century, he plays The Singing Ranger three times on *Theme Time Radio Hour*, each time admiring both Hank's repertoire ("seven numbers one, all conspicuous and distinct, plain and straightforward") and his voice ("he was one of the biggest voices in country music"). In short: in every decade of Dylan's career, Hank Snow passes by. Before that even; "When I was growing up, I had a record called *Hank Snow Sings Jimmie Rodgers*," he says in a 1997 phone interview with Nick Krewen on the occasion of *The Songs of Jimmie Rodgers - A Tribute*, a star-studded tribute album organized by Dylan in celebration of Jimmie Rodgers' 100th birthday.

"One More Night" is musically in the vein of "I'm Moving On" or "Music Making Mama From Tennessee" or "I Wonder Where You Are Tonight" anyway, one of those mid-tempo songs from that endless string (85 titles!) of Hank Snow singles from the first half of the 50s. With an intro that seems to have inspired Neil Young's "Heart Of Gold", by the way (the song of which Dylan says: "There I am, but it's not me").

Strangely, Snow's sharper singing voice is closer to Dylan's voice on *John Wesley Harding* than to the more nasal onset on *Nashville Skyline*, but still it does seem as if the smooth baritone of The Singing Ranger is haunting Dylan's mind here. That's not the most remarkable thing, though. What is particularly striking is Dylan's largely unemotional delivery. In all the other songs on *Nashville Skyline*, we hear Hanks Snow-like tricks to communicate emotion. The near cracking in "To Be Alone With You", the descent into a sultry baritone in "Lay Lady Lay", the light vibrato and the hint of a head voice in "Tonight I'll Be Staying Here With You" and "I Threw It All Away"... the "usual" crooning tricks, as it were. But "One More Night" gets a detached, almost mechanical treatment. The opening lines,

> One more night, the stars are in sight
> But tonight I'm as lonesome as can be

... are, admittedly, not too inspiring, but then again, so are plenty of verses in the other songs, which do get audible love in the delivery. Here, however, Dylan sounds like the jaded country star of old who has to sing his one sole hit from thirty years ago for the umpteenth time at an Oldies festival. An impression that in the last lines, in

> Oh, I miss that woman so
> I didn't mean to see her go

... is squared again; you can just hear how this washed-out country star wonders *what the hell I am doing here*, and is already, while indifferently singing these lines, thinking about the way back to his camper and his bed.

The song can take it, weirdly enough. It is, after all, a skilled, immaculate country song, Dylan is accompanied by skilled, excellent musicians who effortlessly layer an irresistible bounciness under Dylan's drawl, and the familiar melody lines are strong enough to stand on their own, are not necessarily in need of polishing with frills and tinsel.

Just as clichéd, but no less appealing, are the lyrics, with tone, idiom and content of each tear-in-my-beer ballad between

Hank Williams' "Why Don't You Love Me" (1950) and "There's A Tear In My Beer", the late Hank Williams' unique duet with his son Hank Williams Jr. from 1988, lamentations which communicate the same suffering as

> *One more night, the stars are in sight*
> *But tonight I'm as lonesome as can be*
> *Oh, the moon is shinin' bright*
> *Lighting ev'rything in sight*
> *But tonight no light will shine on me*

The only distinguishing feature, as is to be expected from a Nobel Prize-winning poet, is the superior form. Dylan chooses, instinctively presumably, the form he tends to choose for his Very Big Songs, the Spanish sextet (six-line stanzas with the rhyme scheme AABCCB). Concealed, as usual, by an inexplicable intervention by the layout editor, who rearranges all four stanzas into five-line stanzas. But both the rhyme scheme and Dylan's delivery demonstrate that all four stanzas are "actually" Spanish sextets. This first verse, for example, is in fact:

> *One more night,*
> *the stars are in sight*
> *But tonight I'm as lonesome as can be*
> *Oh, the moon is shinin' bright*
> *Lighting ev'rything in sight*
> *But tonight no light will shine on me*

Just as the second verse "actually" is AABCCB, turns out to be a Spanish sextet as well:

> *Oh, it's shameful and it's sad*
> *I lost the only pal I had*
> *I just could not be what she wanted me to be*
> *I will turn my head up high*
> *To that dark and rolling sky*
> *For tonight no light will shine on me*

... revealed through an intervention in the opening line, an intervention that produces the same result in each of the stanzas: Spanish sextets, all of them.

We see it often enough, Dylan's love for this form, the rather rare form of songs like "A Boy Named Sue" and "Hallelujah". Dylan chooses it in exceptional songs like "Love Minus Zero" and "Where Are You Tonight?", always concealing the form in the official publications (*Lyrics* and on the site), as here again, by re-formatting the lyrics.

It remains a mystery why Dylan, or the layout editor, would choose to do that. But it's certainly not middle of the road, in any case.

II   I believe in Hank Williams

While the lyrics may be somewhat distinctive in form, the musical accompaniment is not, nor is there much to enjoy in terms of content. In terms of content, the lyrics offer little or no sparkling poetry or other fireworks; it is mainly a string of country clichés. Starting with the theme, which is probably the trigger for the entire song text: *one more night* - the bittersweet farewell of a love affair. A theme like Kris Kristofferson elaborates on around the same time, much more movingly, in one of his most beautiful songs, in "For The Good Times";

Lay your head upon my pillow
Hold your warm and tender body close to mine
Hear the whisper of the rain drops flowing soft against the window
And make believe you love me one more time
For the good times

A song that would only be catapulted into the stratosphere after *Nashville Skyline,* in the version by Ray Price, who scored a huge hit with it in 1970, after which the song was definitively elevated to the canon by Elvis and Al Green, among others. Kristofferson himself recorded the song in 1970, but maybe Dylan knows Bill Nash's version from 1968.

Or not. "Before You Accuse Me", Ray Charles' "Get On The Right Track Baby", Jimmy Dean's "One Last Time", Hank Williams' "Why Don't You Love Me"... the theme is obviously generic enough to have entered Dylan's repertoire without any immediate cause or current trigger. Bing Crosby's top hit from 1931, "Just One More Chance" even uses literally the same words;

Just one more night
To taste the kisses that enchant me
I'd want no others if you'd grant me
Just one more chance

... as well as plenty of other songs. Oh well, we even hear this word combination in one of The Monkees' most enjoyable songs, in the 1966 world hit "Last Train To Clarksville" - a rather transparent "Paperback Writer" rip-off, but no less enjoyable for that.

'Cause I'm leaving in the morning
And I must see you again
We'll have one more night together
Till the morning brings my train and I must go
Oh, no, no, no
Oh, no, no, no

Much the same applies to Dylan's choice of words in the verses. Dylan has found his lyrics for "One More Night" by browsing through country classics left and right. Although not necessarily in the standards. "Kaw-Liga", for example, echoes in more songs on *Nashville Skyline*, and is actually a rather atypical song in Hank Williams' repertoire. Recorded during Hank's very last recording session, September 23, 1952, the same session that yielded the immortal "Your Cheatin' Heart" and "Take These Chains From My Heart". "Kaw-Liga" was co-written with Fred Rose, has an unusual chord progression, an unusual story (about the wooden statue of an Indian with an unfortunate crush on a "Chocktaw maid over in the Georgia store"), and is the only Williams song with a fade-out.

Yet, or perhaps because of this, the record company sees hit potential. It is the A-side of the first single released after Williams' death (1 January 1953), storms the charts and eventually spends 14 weeks at No.1 on the Billboard Country Chart. And impresses the young Robert Zimmerman, as we can read in Clinton Heylin's *The Double Life of Bob Dylan, Volume 1: A Restless, Hungry Feeling, 1941-1966* (2021):

> "I heard Hank Williams. I think [it was] 'Kaw-Liga', and [the DJ] said he was dead. Hank's voice stopped me in my tracks. It was from the same world as the Stanley [Brothers] but from [a] more focused part of it – it was more explanatory [*sic*] and less mysterious, more jolting and spine-tingling, especially the voice."

Hank Williams' repertoire seems to be etched in the creative part of Dylan's brain, to which we probably owe the jumpiness of the musical accompaniment and the simple poetry of the lyrics of "One More Night" anyway, but we also see it more explicitly. "Tell Me That It Isn't True" varies quite literally on Hank

Williams' "You Win Again", from "Kaw-Liga" a lyric fragment like *"Is it any wonder"* moves to "Tonight I'll Be Staying Here With You" and Hank's refrain

> *Kaw-Liga, ooh*
> *Standin' there, as lonesome as can be*
> *Ah, just wishin' he were still an ol' pine tree*

... echoes in Dylan's opening couplet:

> *One more night, the stars are in sight*
> *But tonight I'm as lonesome as can be*
> *Oh, the moon is shinin' bright*
> *Lighting ev'rything in sight*
> *But tonight no light will shine on me*

In which, of course, we hear more Williams traces. "Wait For The Light To Shine", "I Saw The Light", "Blue Moon Of Kentucky"... this first verse can be cut and pasted from Hank's oeuvre quite effortlessly, as can almost all of the lyrics.

It is, all in all, clear that Dylan is not driven by a thirst for originality. He trusts - rightly so - in the power of the familiar. "My songs, what makes them different is that there's a foundation to them. That's why they're still around, that's why my songs are still being performed. It's not because they're such great songs," says Dylan in 1997, in the interview with Jon Pareles for the New York Times. The same interview in which he says: "Those old songs are my lexicon and my prayer book [...] I believe in Hank Williams singing *I Saw the Light*. I've seen the light, too."

Nevertheless, "One More Night" is neither *"still around"* nor *"still being performed"*. Dylan himself performs the song only once, and not even really. It's 6 June 1990, Dylan is in Toronto, has just played the fourteenth song on the set list and then says:

> "Hero of mine ... Ronnie Hawkins! Where is he? He said he would come up and sing a song ... called *One More Night*. It would be awfully nice if he would come up. If he doesn't want to come up that's okay too! ... All right ... Oh, here he comes now!"

... and then has Ronnie *The Hawk* Hawkins sing "One More Night". A gesture of appreciation, presumably - Hawkins is one of the very few artists to ever record a cover of the song. And was there early; Ronnie's cover is the opening song of his eponymous 1970 solo album, produced by Dylan producer Jerry Wexler, with Duane Allman on guitar. The real highlight is the opening song of Side Two, Hawkins' brilliant cover of Dylan's "One Too Many Mornings", but Ronnie himself apparently thinks "One More Night" is a stronger entrant.

Not exactly an unforgettable performance, but then again, there's nothing wrong with it. And we have to hand it to The Hawk: although he approaches the flatness and the emotionlessness of Dylan's original, he can't suppress a little sob here and a half-breaking of the voice there.

4   Lay Lady Lay (1969)

T Bone Burnett is a fan. A great find is "Just Dropped In" in the performance of Kenny Rogers & The First Edition under the psychedelic trip scene in *The Big Lebowski*. When the popular 'multimedia platform' *Garden & Gun* asks for a 'Smoking Southern Playlist' in 2018, Burnett selects ten songs, with Mickey Newbury's "Nights When I Am Sane" gracing the list among classics like "Wade In The Water" from The Staple Singers and Hoagy Carmichael's "Lazy River". And in January 2019 T Bone comes full circle when he chooses "Just Dropped In" for the ambitious, masterful hit series *True Detective*, this time in a newer version by Mickey Newbury himself (over the credits of season 3, episode 1).

Mickey Newbury is a great artist, though first and foremost a musician's musician, a highly acclaimed songwriter who makes beautiful records and beautiful songs, but his money is mainly earned thanks to the royalties of the covers. Keith Richards, Joan Baez, Johnny Cash, Jerry Lee Lewis, Etta James, Roy Orbison ... not small fry either, the artists who cover his songs. And towering above everything and everyone, of course, is Elvis, who elevates Newbury's "An American Trilogy" to the canon.

Dylan met him at least once, on that memorable evening in the spring of 1969 at Johnny Cash's home, where after dinner some of the world's best songwriters gather around the fireplace:

> I was having dinner at Johnny Cash's house outside of Nashville. There were a lot of songwriters there. Joni Mitchell, Graham Nash, Harlan Howard, Kris Kristofferson, Mickey Newberry [sic] and some others. [...] We sat in a circle and each songwriter would play a song and pass the guitar to the next player. [...] I played "Lay, Lady, Lay" and I passed the guitar to Graham Nash.
> (*Chronicles*)

Graham Nash recalls it slightly differently, of course attributing a leading role to himself again. Johnny Cash instructs his guests to play a song.

> Nobody moved. Bob was sitting on the stairs with Sara, and both of them looked uncomfortable. Mickey Newbury, a famous songwriter from Nashville, was there; so was Kris Kristofferson, and of course Joni and me. Everyone stared at those guitars as if they were radioactive.

But Graham feels 'ridiculously' confident and thinks: *Fuck it – I'll get up.*

> So I grabbed a guitar, sat on the stool, and whipped off a version of "Marrakesh Express". *All abooooard* ... I hit the last chord, knew I'd killed it, put the guitar back on the stand ... and walked right into a standing lamp that went crashing to the floor.
> (*Wild Tales, A Rock & Roll Life*)

Which breaks the ice. Everyone laughs, Dylan overcomes his reticence and plays "Lay Lady Lay" and "Don't Think Twice". Kristofferson does "Sunday Morning Coming Down", Joni Mitchell "Both Sides Now". What Mickey Newbury plays Nash does not disclose, but he has to be given credit for spelling his name correctly, unlike Dylan does.

Newbury's masterpiece *Looks Like Rain* is to be released half a year later, and it is an obvious guess he performs the highlight of that album, the magical folk song "San Francisco Mabel Joy".

The record contains only beautiful songs ("She Even Woke Me Up To Say Goodbye", "The Thirty-Third Of August", to name but two of the most covered ones), but the Dylan fan especially jumps up at "T. Total Tommy". Although the title suggests an ode to the country and bluegrass legend Tom T. Hall, the first verse already makes clear that Newbury targets Dylan:

> *To the sad-eyed misinterpreted*
> *Hung-up child of clay*
> *So the drunken poet's pretty words*
> *Didn't help you find your way*

... and the chorus gives away which style figure from the intimate living room concert resonates with Mickey:

> *T Total Tommy took a toke of tea*
> *Black cats backin' up a big oak tree*
> *Tick tocks ticking out a tune on time*
> *Last words looking for a line to rhyme*
> *Saw fish swimming in the sea-saw-sea*
> *But me, well, I'm only looking*

A frantically alliterating chorus, concluded with a nod to "It's Alright Ma (I'm Only Bleeding)" (the next chorus ends with *I'm only crying*), and in between some more Dylan references and paraphrases.

Newbury has heard Dylan singing *Lay lady lay across my big brass bed* a couple of times and seems to think this intrusive initial rhyming is typically enough to copy into his Dylan pastiche. Understandable, but not quite a direct hit; Alliteration has been a popular figure of style for centuries and every songwriter sooner or later succumbs to it. This same evening, Mickey also hears how Graham Nash's *Colored cottons hang in air / Charming cobras in the square*, that Joni Mitchell sings *And ice cream castles in the air / and feather canyons everywhere*, not to mention the Actual Apostle of Alliteration, Kris Kristofferson:

> <u>W</u>ell I <u>w</u>oke up Sunday morning
> <u>W</u>ith no <u>w</u>ay to <u>h</u>old my <u>h</u>ead, that didn't <u>h</u>urt
> And the <u>b</u>eer I had for <u>b</u>reakfast wasn't <u>b</u>ad

Other, just as little reliable sources say Kristofferson is playing "Me And Bobby McGee" that evening. Makes no difference - that song also has an initial rhyme in almost every line of verse.

Anyway: Newbury associates letter rhyming with Dylan.

Dylan himself attributes the opening words to creative poverty, as he reveals in the *Biograph* booklet. "The song came out of those first four chords. I filled it up with the lyrics then, the la la la type thing, well that turned into *Lay Lady Lay*, it's the same thing with the tongue, that's all it was really."

The continuation, *lay across my big brass bed*, can just as little be attributed to a fresh, original flash:

> I take it to my room and lay it 'cross my big brass bed
> I take it to my room and lay it 'cross my big brass bed
> I guess I'll be my own singer, neighbours turn cherry red

... from "Rough Alley Blues" (1931), from the man who could sing the blues like nobody can, Blind Willie McTell.

Nor can the rest of the lyrics be accused of Nobel worthy *new poetic expressions,* or any other literary shine, for that matter.

Dylan himself is not too content with it either, according to the same *Biograph* commentary. Columbia Records president Clive Davis wants to release the song as a single. "I begged and pleaded with him not to. I never felt too close to the song, or thought it was representative of anything I do."

In interviews he makes similar remarks ("There may be better singles in the fresh material," Melody Maker, August 1969), and also more precise ones:

> I rewrote "Lay, Lady, Lay", too.. (...) A lot of words to that song have changed. I recorded it originally surrounded by a bunch of other songs on the *Nashville Skyline* album. That was the tone of the session. Once everything was set, that was the way it came out. And it was fine for that time, but I always had a feeling there was more to the song than that.
>
> (*Playboy* interview, November 1977)

Whether Dylan has indeed found more in the song is debatable. During the *Rolling Thunder Revue* and in the *Hard Rain* version, a few lines have changed, that much is true. A hollow cliché like *You can have your cake and eat it too* has been replaced by the not much stronger *You can love, but you might lose it*, for example (but resurfaces on other nights on other places in the song). On *Hard Rain* a total of 78 (out of 171) words are different, so yes, okay, *a lot of words have changed*. And: those performances are done with an overwhelming extra shot of love, with energy and a compelling urgency - and that certainly benefits the song.

The alleged missing warmth or representativeness is not that big an issue anymore, evidently; Dylan has played the song more than 400 times, plays it still in the twenty-first century, pushing "Lay Lady Lay" into his personal Top 50.

Enough colleagues who feel warmth for the song, too. "Lay Lady Lay" has fans like Madonna, The Everly Brothers and Duran Duran, apparently touching more artists than just the usual suspects like The Byrds, Richie Havens or Melanie. Many more artists even; the song is probably in a (non-existing) Top 20 of most covered Dylan songs.

Magnet's fascinating, atmospheric version (with a wonderful guest contribution by Gemma Hayes, for the soundtrack of *Mr. & Mrs. Smith*, 2005) is rightly praised. The industrial grunge approach by Ministry is distinctive, to say the least (on *Filth Pig*, 1996) and actually has the Lure of the Forbidden.

But in the end, a laid-back, sultry approach fits the song best. Like Buddy Guy (*Bring 'Em In*, 2005) or the one by Cher (for safety reasons changed to "Lay *Baby* Lay"), on her exquisite, staggeringly disregarded album *3614 Jackson Highway* (1969), produced in the well-known Muscle Shoals Studio, Sheffield Alabama, by grandmaster Jerry Wexler.

The ultimate swoon away version should, obviously, have come from Barry White, but The Walrus Of Love breaches his duties. He is excellently replaced by Isaac Hayes though, on the beautiful tribute album *Tangled Up In Blues*, 1999. Somewhat over the sultriest top, yes, but for once, only this one time, it is allowed.

5 Western Road

I They wanted to record everything in case Dylan said something profound

Well I'm going to Chicago, going on the Western Road
Yes I'm going to Chicago, going on the Western Road
There are good times in Baltimore
But I've packed this heavy load

It is clearly an improvised cooling down, the trifle "Western Road", the "outtake" we received as an unexpected gift, just like that, on the release of *The Bootleg Series Vol. 15 1967-1969: Travelin' Thru* (2019). The song bubbles up at the end of the second recording session for *Nashville Skyline*, 13 February 1969. From six p.m. to midnight, Dylan, bassist Charlie McCoy and drummer Kenny Buttrey, assisted by Bob Wilson on piano and four alternating guitarists, have been busy putting the final versions of "I Threw It All Away", "To Be Alone With You" and "One More Night" on tape, plus four attempts to capture the beauty of "Lay, Lady, Lay", and now we're pretty much ready to call it a day. But then someone serves up another nightcap.

"Take 1 (Outtake)", as it is somewhat overly ambitiously catalogued on CD1 of this episode of *The Bootleg Series*, begins abruptly, when the first bars have already been played. Remarkable, since producer Bob Johnston has a habit of *always* having a tape running when Dylan is in the studio (to which we also owe the invaluable *The Bootleg Series 12 - The Cutting Edge 1965-1966*). A quirk confirmed again in 2016 by one directly involved, by Bob Wilson, the pianist of the *Nashville Skyline* sessions, being interviewed on a panel with Charlie Daniels and Ron Cornelius, among others, on the occasion of the release of Cornelius' book *The Guitar Behind Dylan & Cohen*:

> "They rolled the tape constantly. And they'd run the tape machine on high speed, 30 ips instead of the usual, you know half of that speed. It's a higher fidelity, but it also ate the tape up. They had stacks of tape lined up. I mean, they had the engineers moving them tapes in and out... 'cause they ate all that tape up, they recorded everything. All the time the machine was running, which was very, very unusual, very rare – they didn't do it that way. So, consequently, the red light was on all the time. So what they wanted, what Bob Johnston wanted, if Dylan said something, they wanted to record everything in case Dylan said something profound [*audience laughter*]."

So those first bars of "Western Road" must also be on a tape somewhere. But for the official release, the first seconds have been cut out; presumably it took a little while before the originator was followed, whoever that might have been. That same pianist, Bob Wilson, would be an educated guess; "Western Road" is musically a copy of Wilson's "After Hours", the B-side of his not very successful single "Suzy's Serenade". It is, of course, only a run-of-the-mill 12 bar blues, so both "Western Road" and "After Hours" are copies of a billion other blues songs, but still - Wilson plays exactly the same runs with his right hand, the key is neighborly (now C major, after the G major of "After Hours"), the groove is identical, albeit the tempo is slightly slower.

And it sort of ignites Dylan. "Unleashed" would perhaps be a too overenthusiastic characterisation, but he does shake, with apparent ease, tolerable lyrics out of his immaculate white shirt sleeve. Very deeply he does not dive into his stream-of-consciousness, though. "Going to Chicago" bubbles up rather smoothly as (presumably) Bob Wilson deploys a Chicago blues. Any research hasn't been done, evidently; if you take the Western Road from Baltimore, you're heading northeast - away from Chicago, that is. Unwise, especially if you *"packed this heavy load"*. As such, it's a dead end. Dylan sticks to Baltimore and Chicago for another verse, but his head is clearly already very much elsewhere, much further west:

> *Might take a train I might take a plane*
> *But if I have to walk*
> *I'll be going to Chicago just the same*
> *I'm going to Chicago on the Western Road*
> *There's bad times in Baltimore I can't take this load*

Dylan has already sung "*I'm going to...*" twice, and now no longer resists the words that then inevitably impose themselves on a walking jukebox:

> *Well I might take a train I might take a plane,*
> *But if I have to walk I'm going just the same*
> *I'm going to Kansas City, Kansas City here I come*
> *They got some crazy lil' women there*
> *And I'm gonna get me one*

... the third verse of one of the all-time great rock songs of the 20th century, Leiber and Stoller's "Kansas City". A song that apparently continues to bounce around in the creative part of Dylan's brain through the decades. It is just short of "One For My Baby (And One More For The Road)", the Sinatra song that echoes in at least seven Dylan songs, but "Kansas City" also comes a long way. It is the song from which Dylan lovingly steals in 1965 for "Just Like Tom Thumb's Blues" (*they got some hungry women there* is a little disguised derivation of Wilbert Harrison's *they got some crazy women there*), and in 2001 for "High Water" (*He made it to Kansas City, Twelfth Street and Vine* is literally copied). He himself plays it once in between, in - of course - Kansas City, when Tom Petty's band is backing him, 24 July 1986. "Well. That's the first time I've ever played that. Well anyway, we know where we are," he says contentedly after the final chord. And as a DJ, in the twenty-first century on his radio show *Theme Time Radio Hour*, he can't ignore the monument either, in Episode 20, "Musical Maps":

> "Here's a chart-topping smash by Mr. Wilbert Harrison, recorded for Bobby Robinson in 1959, and features the barbed-wire guitar of Wild Jimmy Spruill. Y'all know this song, and it always sounds good. Wilbert Harrison. Kansas City."

The song is, in short, unstoppable when an improvising Dylan accidentally sings *"I'm going to..."* over a spontaneous Chicago blues at the end of a recording day in Nashville.

But soon he will return to Baltimore...

II   Ridin' in a buggy, Miss Mary Anne

Peggy Seeger has many merits, obviously, and deserves to be knighted for her own contributions to music history as well, but surely her main claim to fame is and remains that she inspired Ewan MacColl to write "The First Time Ever I Saw Your Face". Which is perhaps somewhat ironic, given her decades-long fight for women's rights and her feminist fire, but presumably she herself would be at peace with that feat; Peggy, above all, has an unshakeable respect for *songs*. And "The First Time Ever I Saw Your Face" is, after all, an indestructible song from the stratosphere. Heck, she even named her own autobiography after the song. *And* she loved Ewan MacColl, let's not forget that.

Her love for Dylan seems to run a little less deep. The story that both Joan Baez and Bob Dylan stalked her for an autograph in 1961 is amusing though not very watertight, and by now belongs to folklore. As is the story that both MacColl and Peggy, who may indeed both be labelled folksnobs, would have felt and expressed disdain for Dylan. In Howard Sounes' *Down The Highway* (2001), she recalls Dylan's visit in December '62 to the club MacColl and she ran in London, The Singers Club in Holborn;

> "He seemed lost without a microphone, as plenty of U.S.A. performers did in our nonwired clubs. Ewan and I were rather standoffish at that time and perhaps we were not welcoming enough."

Twenty years later, in the magazine *Uncut* on the occasion of Dylan's 80th birthday, she tries to nuance her unwelcoming attitude slightly, but is not too successful at that:

> "Not long after, he came to the UK and performed at the Singers Club. But nobody could hear him because we didn't have microphones and his voice wasn't loud enough. Some people have since said that he was given the cold shoulder, but I don't think that's true. It was just that at that time we were singing pretty much folk songs or highly political songs in our club. Bob Dylan's songs fell halfway in between. It was a new kind of song."

However, other sources such as the also present Martin Carthy, A.L. Lloyd and Anthea Joseph could apparently hear it just fine and all recall, independently, that Dylan played "Masters Of War", "Blowin' In The Wind" and presumably an early version of "Ballad Of Hollis Brown". It does look a bit as if Peggy, as the daughter of musicologist Charles and composer Ruth, sister of Mike Seeger and half-sister of Pete Seeger, and partner of Ewan MacColl, sixty years on still is having some trouble admitting that she at the time did not recognise the extraordinary, earth-shattering power of three of Dylan's all-time greatest songs while she was standing next to them. Like in her autobiography *First Time Ever* (2017), where she makes no mention of the not insignificant music-historical fact of Dylan's repeated visits to her club and the subsequent creation of songs like "Hard Rain" and "Girl Of The North Country". Indeed, Dylan is not mentioned at all. Well alright, one time, quite indirectly though, when she recounts with slightly awkward smugness how she manages to get out from under a fine. In a rather implausibly embellished anecdote:

> "A handsome young policeman sticks his head in the window and asks if I know how fast I was going. My Maggie could indeed gallop at full tilt. I admit that I only glanced at the speedometer when I saw the blue lights. 95 mph on a 65 mph road. *No, officer, I'm a musician and I'm very sorry and I was writing a song in my head and I wasn't paying attention* and his

face lights up. *I write songs too! What's your song about?* Off we went, commiserating on the difficulties of putting thoughts and emotions into verse and melody. *You play folk music? Do you know Bobby Dylan and Joanie Baez?* He was impressed that before they were Bobby and Joanie they'd both asked for my autograph, but he zipped back to our songs. He just wanted some tips. He let me off with a warning."

Yes, the Realm of Fantasy is a very nice place to dwell, filled with Things That Never Happened. Unfortunately, Peggy Seeger's memoir is larded with this kind of blatantly pumped up reveries.

Anyway, vice versa, there has always been respect and admiration. In interviews and in his autobiography *Chronicles*, Dylan usually mentions her among names like Bill Monroe and Jean Ritchie, artists he enjoyed listening to. Indeed, songs that are in Peggy's repertoire in the early 1960s can be heard throughout Dylan's oeuvre. "The Wagoner's Lad", "Pretty Saro", "Girl Of Constant Sorrow", "The Death Of Queen Jane", "Railroad Bill"... and again in this third verse of "Western Road";

> *Have you seen, have you seen, have you seen Miss Mary Anne?*
> *Have you seen, have you seen, have you seen Miss Mary Anne?*
> *Well I want to tell you that's one kind of woman, who is missing her man*

The engine falters, by the sound of it. On the spot, Dylan decides to start the third stanza with *"Have you seen..."* but then his improvisational skills let him down for a moment. In haste, he fills the bars with a double repeat of *have you seen*, and then the associations lead him via *"Baltimore"* from both previous stanzas to *"Miss Mary Anne"*, which must have been prompted by Seeger:

> *Ridin' in a buggy, Miss Mary Jane, Miss Mary Jane*
> *I've got a house in Baltimore, in Baltimore, in Baltimore*
> *I've got a house in Baltimore, and it's full of chicken pie*

... "Ridin' In A Buggy", the old folksong/nursery rhyme that has been in Seeger's repertoire since the 1950s. The purist Peggy would presumably raise her finger at Dylan's name change (from "Miss Mary Jane" to "Miss Mary Anne"), but then probably accept Dylan's obvious excuse - after all, during the 1960s, "Mary Jane" has become an insider's wink at marijuana. Or actually already no longer an "insider's wink", but almost colloquial language; even The Everly Brothers sing it on their under-appreciated 1967 flop *The Everly Brothers Sing*:

> *Clouds so sweet, cloud my mind girl*
> *And I don't know, what way I'll go girl*
> *But I don't care no more*
> *I've got my Mary Jane*
> *And I'm secure once more*
> *I've got my Mary Jane*

"Mary Jane", the trippy opening of Side B, and like most songs on the record an admittedly overproduced (it's 1967, after all), but otherwise fine song. The decision to release it on single, hoping to attract a new, hipper audience is defensible (but sadly failed miserably).

Dylan, incidentally, would quote Peggy's "Ridin' In A Buggy" more correctly and respectfully some 30 years later, on *Time Out Of Mind*, in "Tryin' To Get To Heaven"; *I was riding in a buggy with Miss Mary-Jane / Miss Mary-Jane got a house in Baltimore*.

Anyway, today, on this late Thursday evening 13 February 1969 in Nashville, it seems more than likely that Dylan's feverishly meandering brain arrives at "Miss Mary Anne" via *Baltimore* - although the proximity of Johnny Cash could also be a trigger, of course. And that his "The Blizzard" from *Sings The Ballads Of The True West* (1965) bubbles up, the tragic countdown song of the traveller who is seven miles, five miles, three miles, one mile away from his beloved Mary Anne, only to be found frozen to death the next morning... *He was just a hundred yards from Mary Anne*. On the other hand: that's no "Miss".

Either way, she is not a keeper. Either a tired Dylan loses concentration, or he regrets the name choice after just one verse, as she has been renamed already in the next, last verse of this improvised trifle:

> *Look down the street on Friday and found out she was gone*
> *I looked for her on Thursday but she has moved along*
> *Miss Maggie Anne, has anybody seen Miss Maggie Anne?*
> *Well let me tell you that's one woman*
> *One woman who's sure missing her man*

The well is starting to dry up. Half-heartedly, Dylan seems to want to quickly improvise a countdown song, or at least a countdown couplet, one of those that count down the weekdays. An easy way out, though often enough it makes for wonderful songs. "Re-Enlistment Blues" by Merle Travis from 1953, for instance, Etta James's irresistible "Seven Day Fool" (1961), "Stormy Monday" and "Friday On My Mind". And "I Got Stripes", of course, by the inevitable Johnny Cash, lovingly stolen from Lead Belly's upbeat prison song "On A Monday" from '39.

But Dylan seems to have exhausted his resources. After one line he has already lost count (going from *Friday* to *Thursday*), after the second line *Mary Anne* has changed to *Maggie Anne*, and after three lines Dylan has lost the storyline: the untraceable Maggie/Mary Anne who has just run off to the dismay of the abandoned narrator, suddenly is the abandoned one herself in the last line: *that's one woman who's sure missing her man.*

Yeah well, who cares. "Western Road" is just an unserious throwaway anyway. But 50 years later it does give Dylanologists a nice, fleeting glimpse into the inner jukebox of a Nobel Prize-winning grandmaster. Which in itself is a merit, still.

Friday, February 14, 1969
6:00-9:00 pm, and 9:00-midnight

Studio A
Columbia Recording Studios
Nashville, Tennessee
Produced by Bob Johnston

Take 1 – 3
Peggy Day

Take 4 – 11
Tell Me That It Isn't True

Take 12 – 13
Country Pie

Take 14 – 18
Lay, Lady, Lay

Musicians:
Charlie McCoy (bass), Charlie Daniels (guitar and dobro), Kenneth Buttrey (drums), Norman L. Blake (guitar), Robert S. Wilson (piano and organ), Pete Drake (steel guitar) and Kelton D. Herston (probably guitar) 9-12: and Wayne Moss (guitar).

6 Peggy Day

I The head of the snake

In the autumn of 1967, the Big Pink in Woodstock has exotic visitors: The Bauls of Bengal. Manager Albert Grossman had met the troubadour family in Calcutta and invited the men to America. We see two of them, the brothers Purnan and Luxman Das (or: Purna and Lakhsman), flanking Dylan in the cover photo of *John Wesley Harding*. Dylan reportedly enjoyed hanging out with them, calling himself, according to Purnan in an interview with *The Telegraph India* in 1995, "an American Baul".

The funniest anecdote comes from Levon Helm, who in his autobiography *This Wheel's On Fire* (1993) reports on a pleasant evening sharing a good joint with Luxman. "Good weed," Levon says appreciatively to Luxman.

> "Very good, but nothing like my father used to smoke—little hashish, little tobacco, little head of snake."
> I said, "Wait a minute. Did you say 'snake head'?"
> And Luxman laughed. "Yes, by golly! Chop off head of snake, chop into tiny pieces, put in chillum with little hash, little tobacco. Oh, boy! Very good—first-class high!"
> "Snake?" I pressed him. "Are you sure you mean snake?"
> Now they're all laughing. "Yes! Very good! Head of snake!"

It is a wonderful anecdote with a high Monty Python quality. Michael Palin as Luxman, and the role of Levon Helm should, of course, be played by John Cleese. In terms of content, it is already strong because of the absurdity of the plot, and stylistically because of Luxman's naturalness and perfect timing (*first* hash, *then* tobacco, and finally "little head of snake"), and especially because of his use of language - the combination of broken sentences with brutal imperatives ("chop off head") and corny idioms like "oh, boy" and particularly "by golly" is irresistible.

Dylan, the language-sensitive word artist, will have saved it somewhere, only to put it in the right place about a year later, when he has "Peggy Day" up his sleeve:

> *Peggy Day stole my poor heart away*
> *By golly, what more can I say*
> *Love to spend the night with Peggy Day*

Initially, the album and the song are received with some goodwill. It sells well, "Lay Lady Lay" becomes a big hit and reviews are friendly. Like in Newsweek (*"Peggy Day" is almost a pastiche of the Thirties - its rhythms recall "swing" and Dylan sings with the kind of light-hearted showmanship that used to come from college bandstands*) and in New Musical Express, 19 April 1969:

> "In the final track on side one, Dylan makes it abundantly clear he'd like to spend the night with 'Peggy Day'. Eminently hummable, and probably the 'Ob-La-Di Ob-La-Da' of 'Nashville Skyline'. The guitars chatter away, a pedal guitar break, and a rousing blues climax."

Time, or rather: professional Dylanologists are not too kind on the charming little ditty "Peggy Day". Clinton Heylin calls the song "embarrassing", Howard Sounes finds it "vacuous", Mike

Marqusee catalogues it as "an exercise in deliberate banality", and Ian Bell feels little affection for it either: "Possibly the poorest song Dylan had sanctioned for release since his earliest apprentice days." Shelton is still the kindest: "Dylan has some fun with the clichés of country and country-music whimsy on *Peggy Day*."

In fan circles, the song, like the entire *Nashville Skyline* album, is in the yo-yo category. Burned down and slammed, until an undercurrent of fans hoist "Peggy Day" up on a shield and then, without too much justification, appreciate the "irony" or alleged double meanings or – quite on the contrary - the purity. And when the undercurrent becomes an overcurrent, the opposing forces mobilise again, and the process starts all over again. More or less the same dynamic as in the appreciation of, for example, *Street-Legal*, "Make You Feel My Love" and *Saved*.

On the other side of the divide are fans like Elvis Costello ("the songs sounded like great Tin Pan Alley tunes to me, especially my favourite cut, *Peggy Day*") and Nick Cave, for whom *Nashville Skyline* is the all-time favourite album.

The negative comments are - obviously - from the disappointted ones, from the fans who use reference points like "Visions Of Johanna" and "Tangled Up In Blue". Still, the song itself is not *that* bad; "Peggy Day" is an unambitious piece of craftsmanship by a Song and Dance Man - no more, but certainly no less.

The first bars make that clear right away; a fairly generic chord progression, F - D7 - Gm - C7, a progression we know from dozens of songs, from "Maxwell's Silver Hammer" to "Can't Take My Eyes Off Of You", from "Stars Fell On Alabama" to Patsy Cline's

"Crazy", and from "Georgia On My Mind" to The Lovin' Spoonful's "Daydream" - just to name a few. And just as generic are the opening lyrics;

> *Peggy Day stole my poor heart away*

... a protagonist who self-pitifully laments *"my poor heart"* is known not from dozens, but from hundreds of songs. And a considerable number of those can be found in Dylan's personal jukebox. Big Bill Broonzy's "Southbound Train", for example, and "Trouble In Mind", "I Got It Bad (And That Ain't Good)", "Don't Blame Me", "You Are My Sunshine", "Wildwood Flower", and "The Sky Is Crying"... the chances of hitting a *my poor heart* while pressing any button on the jukebox with your eyes closed are pretty good.

Dylan himself probably prefers, especially here and now in Nashville, to sing along with his hero George Jones, who sings "Time Changes Everything" (*When you left me my poor heart was broken*) on the tribute album to another of Dylan's heroes, *George Jones Sings Bob Wills* from 1962. Or with Hank Williams' "We Live in Two Different Worlds" (*Oh how my poor heart will pine*). Or in the song that will form a blueprint for Dylan's late masterpiece "Red River Shore", Gene Autry's version of "Red River Valley" from 1946, or in the song that Dylan also has in his repertoire in the early 60s, in "Handsome Molly" (*My poor heart is aching / You are at your ease*).

Bob Wills, George Jones, Hank Williams, Gene Autry... none of Dylan's greatest country heroes are ashamed of the tearful, melodramatic *my poor heart*. So Dylan will certainly not feel too big for it either. But the disappointed ones may indeed regret that the song and dance man doesn't wrap that poor heart in a frenzied rhyming verse with vicious outbursts. Like that other Greatest Songwriter of the Twentieth Century, Cole Porter, does:

> *My poor heart is achin'*
> *To bring home some bacon*
> *And if I find myself alone and forsaken*
> *It's simply because I'm the laziest gal in town*

"The Laziest Gal in Town", one of those boisterous rhyming brilliants by grandmaster Cole Porter. Often recorded and often performed, but rarely as breath-taking as by Marlene Dietrich in her white negligee in Hitchcock's *Stage Fright* from 1950.

La Dietrich is still defeated though, by the way. Fourteen years later, by the lady who stands on a marble pedestal with Dylan as well, by Nina Simone.

Yes, by golly.

II   A benevolent appearance

The Father of a Murderer is the last book the successful German author Alfred Andersch (1914-1980) completed, just before his death. It is a short, autobiographical story (96 pages) that masterfully recounts the last lesson of Andersch's alter ego Franz Kien at the Wittelsbacher Gymnasium in Munich.

In May 1928, the start of Greek class is startled by the entry of "the Rex", rector Himmler, who comes to "inspect" the class.

Himmler, indeed the father of Heinrich Himmler, is a massive, terrifying presence who soon takes over the class. His secret agenda becomes clear halfway through the lesson; not so much class inspection, as clean-up. And one of the victims is the poorly performing Franz. Andersch knows how to compellingly evoke the oppression that descends on the pupils - they know that Himmler will soon call someone to the blackboard to be gutted in front of the entire class. And Himmler knows that they know - and plays with the rising fear like a cat with its mouse.

When Franz is finally called up, Himmler tells him to write down the sentence *"It is deserving to praise Franz Kien"* in Greek on the blackboard. Franz, a lazy and uninterested pupil comes, of course, to nothing. Himmler must help him with every letter. "You," judges the Rex after ten torturous minutes, "you will not qualify for the Upper Secondary." Franz shrugs his shoulders.

> The good thing about that is that he will then stop examining me and call someone else to the blackboard. If I'm going to fail anyway, he doesn't need to examine me anymore.
> "It is not deserving to praise Franz Kien," said the Rex.
> Cheap, thought Franz, this had to come. Only because he can invert the sentence and throw back at me he picked it out in the first place.

It did in fact more or less play out like this with Alfred Andersch. Andersch really was a pupil at that Wittelsbacher Gymnasium as a fourteen-year-old boy and was actually expelled from school by Himmler's father, Joseph Gebhard Himmler. But Alfred/Franz is lazy, not stupid. He is a keen observer, sees through character flaws in both his teacher and Himmler, and thinks quickly. Like he does here: "Cheap. Only because he can invert the sentence and throw back at me he picked it out in the first place."

Franz Kien would undoubtedly think exactly the same if he heard the second verse of "Peggy Day":

> *Peggy night makes my future look so bright*
> *Man, that girl is out of sight*
> *Love to spend the day with Peggy night*

... the reversal from *love to spend the night with Peggy Day* to *love to spend the day with Peggy night* is, after all, as corny as you can get. Well, cheap even. "Only because he can invert the name he picked it out in the first place."

Although it could also be a by-catch; in choosing the name for his protagonist, Dylan seems to be driven by the ambition to be as kitschy as possible. And then he comes up with a rather unimaginative combination of *Doris Day* and *Peggy Lee*, something like that. Not unfathomable; Peggy Lee is a 40s/50s icon anyway, having just returned to the spotlight with a Grammy for "Is That All There Is?" (1969), and the star of Doris Day, that other 40s/50s icon, is suddenly shining again thanks to the successful television series *The Doris Day Show*.

As in the opening couplet, however, the easy-going lyricist still adds some irony. Just as Dylan inserted the anachronistic *"by golly"* before this, he now chooses the equally alienating *"out of sight"*. In 1969, this is a rather fresh, hip metaphor to express something like "awesome", ill-suited to the conservative Peggy Lee/Doris Day cut of the surrounding lines. After all, up to and including the 1950s, "out of sight" literally meant "too far to be seen, not visible". But presumably only since 1963, since James Brown's "Out Of Sight" (*You're more than alright / You know you're out of sight*) has it been used to describe the physical attractiveness of a lady or awesomeness in general.

Stevie Wonder then takes it outside soul circles in 1965 with the mega hit "Uptight" (*Baby, everything is all right, uptight, out of sight*). Admittedly, at first hearing a little awkward and unintentionally ironic when sung by the blind Stevie Wonder (who also sings "I'm the apple of my girl's eye" a little further on), but he did not write this part of the lyrics himself. Stevie had the riff, the music and the opening words "everything is all right, uptight", Sylvia Moy completed the lyrics.

And the Easybeats eventually spread the new, hip metaphor all over the planet with their 1967 world hit, "Friday On My Mind";

> *Gonna have fun in the city*
> *Be with my girl, she's so pretty*
> *She looks fine tonight*
> *She is out of sight to me*

Alienating in a very conservative country-shuffle like "Peggy Day" pretends to be, but on the other hand: Dylan also seems to be aiming for a *cringe-factor*, for the awkwardness that the adolescent experiences when his mother uses the wrong abbreviations in her apps and his father starts replying with memes. And Dylan succeeds, too; first the stale "by golly", and now the hip, youthful *"Man, that girl is out of sight"*... a harmless dork, you'd think. But then again, so does the old Himmler appear;

> There was something sparkling, lively and now benevolent, apparently warmly affectionate in the brightly reddened face under smooth white hair, but Franz immediately had the impression that the Rex, although he could give himself a benevolent appearance, was not harmless; his friendliness was certainly not to be trusted, not even now, when he looked, jovially and portly, at the pupils sitting in three double rows in front of him.

Franz has a keen eye. And we also know by now, since *Shadow Kingdom* in 2021, what horrors Dylan hid under "To Be Alone With You", under another seemingly harmless ditty on *Nashville Skyline*. Who knows what will happen when Dylan reanimates "Peggy Day".

> His tone was no longer affable. The father of the school, looking benignly after one of his classes - that was now definitely over; up there, behind the desk as if on a perch, now sat a hunter.

III   This record tears out your backbone

Paris Jackson, Michael's daughter, is very angry. "I'm so incredibly offended by it, as i'm sure plenty of people are as well, and it honestly makes me want to vomit," she tweets on Wednesday 11 January 2017. The outburst doesn't relieve her as yet; moments later, she twitters on: "it angers me to see how obviously intentional it was for them to be this insulting, not just towards my father, but my godmother liz as well." And nephew Taj Jackson also chips in: "No words could express the blatant disrespect." The anger has been triggered by, incredibly, the honourable Ralph Fiennes. Specifically, by the makers of the terrific Sky Arts series *Urban Myths*, who have announced the airing of the episode "Elizabeth, Michael and Marlon", a light-hearted portrayal of an alleged road-trip taken by Marlon Brando, Elizabeth Taylor and Michael Jackson. The in itself intriguing fact that the King of Pop is played by the *white* Ralph Fiennes proves unpalatable.

Sky Arts is discouraged by all the fuss, and cancels the episode, sadly. The controversy somewhat overshadows the success of the series. A week after the shitstorm on Twitter, on 19 January 2017, is the broadcast of the first episode, that will turn out to be one of the most successful: "Knockin' On Dave's Door". Which is a "true-ish" staging of the apocryphal story of Dylan visiting Dave Stewart in London in 1987, but ringing the wrong doorbell. The lady who opens the door does not recognise him and says "Dave" has been called away. This Dave is, of course, another Dave altogether. Bob gets a cuppa tea and is allowed to wait for "Dave" in the front room. The episode is packed with small, witty, well-documented references to Dylan's biography, and here in the front room the next one follows: Billy Lee Riley, Dylan's rockabilly hero.

"Dylan" (great role by Eddie Marsan) rummages through the record collection, finds a Billy Lee Riley LP and soon "Red Hot" is blaring through the small working-class house at 145 Crouch Hill. Ange, the lady of the house, enters to check on things.

"This record tears out your backbone and kinda makes you feel grateful that it did all at the same time!" shouts "Dylan" above the music, a beautiful paraphrase of Dylan's actual words in the MusiCares Speech, 2015:

> "So Billy became what is known in the industry – a condescending term, by the way – as a one-hit wonder. But sometimes, just sometimes, once in a while, a one-hit wonder can make a more powerful impact than a recording star who's got 20 or 30 hits behind him. And Billy's hit song was called "Red Hot," and it was red hot. It could blast you out of your skull and make you feel happy about it. Change your life. He did it with power and style and grace."

Ange can also appreciate Billy Lee. Still: "It's a great album, yes, but I prefer *No Name Girl*." Bob looks at Ange for a moment, then turns off "Red Hot", closes his eyes and sings "The girl I got ain't got no name." Amused, Ange sings along, which takes us to the bridge of "Peggy Day":

> *The girl I love ain't got no name*
> *But I love her just the same*
> *She's a little peculiar but it ain't no sin*
> *She never know where she going but know were she's been*

... and Dylan sighs in conclusion: "Oh man, he was a real deal."

The bridge of "Peggy Day" offers, at least in terms of content, the only peculiar verse of the song;

> *Well, you know that even before I learned her name*
> *You know I loved her just the same*
> *An' I tell 'em all, wherever I may go*
> *Just so they'll know, that she's my little lady*
> *And I love her so*

... insinuating that the name *Peggy Day* is so overwhelming that you inevitably fall in love with its bearer - but as it so happens, Peggy is lovely to such an inconceivable extent that I fell in love with her *even before I learned her name*. Peculiar. Nameless ladies are often enough sung about, and usually it is considered a factor that contributes to the attractiveness of the lady. Adding to her mysteriousness, something like that. The best known is probably "The French Girl" by Ian & Sylvia, a song for which Dylan has an abiding fascination. He played it in '67 in the Basement, rehearsed it in 1987 with the Grateful Dead (but eventually cut it from the set list), the French girl appears in "Stuck Inside Of Mobile", and twenty years later again in "Dark Eyes". And she never gets a name, in line with Ian Tyson's primal French Girl;

> *So you may find above the border*
> *A girl with silver rings, I never knew her name*
> *You're bound to lose, she's too much for you*
> *She'll leave you lost one rainy morn, you won't be the same*

A beautiful, melancholic song, by the way, which somehow Dylan just can't get hold of. The unforgettable Gene Clark does a better job - especially on the stereo remix of 1991, from which the hideous backing vocals from the mono original of 1967 have fortunately been radically cut out.

Anyway, there are many ladies who, like their male counterpart *tall dark stranger*, apparently become all the more exciting when we don't know her name. "East Virginia Blues", the song Dylan will play with Earl Scruggs in May 1970 (*There I met the fairest maiden and her name I did not know*), The Stones' "Silver Train", Thin Lizzy's "Cowboy Song"... but the superlative is, obviously, Steve Winwood's indestructible masterpiece for Traffic, "No Face, No Name, No Number" (1967).

Dylan himself has also been toying around with that sought-after mystery of anonymity before, in "Outlaw Blues" (1965);

> *I got a woman in Jackson,*
> *I ain't gonna say her name*
> *She's a brown-skin woman,*
> *But I love her just the same*

... where it is of course striking that Dylan uses an identical line in "Peggy Day" to arrive at the rhyme; *"I loved her just the same"* versus *"I love her just the same"*. It reinforces the impression that the illogic of the bridge is due to uninspired rhyming, cutting and pasting by an improvising Dylan. Indeed, in both takes, the official one from *Nashville Skyline* and the first take found on CD1 of *Travelin' Thru: The Bootleg Series Vol. 15 1967-1969* (2019), we hear Dylan stumble and hesitate a bit, and both versions deviate from the published lyrics in the same place;

> *Well you know ever even before I learned her name*

... he sings on *Nashville Skyline*. Or in the first take on *Travelin' Thru*:

> *Well you know ever since before I learned her name*

Clumsy. And just as clumsy, in fact, as rhyming with Billy Lee Riley's *"I loved her just the same"* - a phrase used only to express "but still". Like in Deep Purple's "Hush" (*She broke my heart but I love her just the same*), in Conway Twitty's "Hey Miss Ruby" (*She don't love me but I love her just the same*), in The Everly Brothers' heck of a melodrama "Rockin' Alone" (*The ones who forgot her she loves just the same*), and in Dylan's own "Outlaw Blues", not least - just to name a few. Always songs, anyway, where the "I love her just the same" phrasing communicates a perfectly logical "yet"-message. More coherent than this weird variation in "Peggy Day", the variation that seems to want to express in a failed way that it was love at first sight, that Peggy had already stolen my heart before I got to know her.

Yeah well, Dylan seems to think, while stumbling over his words. It's just an album filler. I'll never play it again anyhow. But just to be sure, he steers back to safe, uncomplicated country clichés to complete the bridge. *"My little lady"* from Jimmie Rodgers' "My Rough And Rowdy Ways", *"I love her so"* from thousands of songs, a snippet of Stanley Brothers (*wherever I may go* from "Riding That Midnight Train")... no, this one won't earn him a Nobel Prize. But what the heck.

IV Hobbling the opposition

"If a Martian came to Earth tomorrow and asked me, Cliff, how many iconic rock and roll songs have you made? I would say, One – *Move It*." Cliff Richard is not exactly blessed with the literary talent of a Dylan or even a Keith Richards ("A Martian"? Couldn't any earthling from, say, old Honolulu or Ashtabula ask the same question?), but still, his autobiography *The Dreamer* (2020) is entertaining, pleasantly modest and, well, charming. And he cherishes John Lennon's comment about his "only iconic rock and roll song";

> "A few years later, John Lennon was kind enough to say: "Before Cliff and "Move It", there was nothing worth listening to in British music" (*you have to admit – he has great taste!*). I was flattered by the comment – and I still am. Being called the first British rock and roller by such a legendary musician is an honour that I will take to my grave."

"Living Doll", on the other hand, says Sir Cliff, "was a weak, pseudo-rock song," but contractually he has to release a song from his debut film *Serious Charge* on single. Shadows guitarist Bruce Welch manages to overcome Cliff's reluctance: "'Why not do it another way?' He picked at a few chords. 'Why not do it as ... a country song?'"

The Beatles appear often enough in Cliff's autobiography; Richard describes an amicable cameraderie. There are no links to The Stones, though. Except once, when Cliff "by mistake" scores a hit with a Jagger/Richards song;

> "The tape didn't have any songwriters' names on it but we thought it was a nice song, and would suit me and The Shadows, so we shifted it from the 'Maybe' to the 'Yes' pile. It wasn't until after we recorded it that we knew it had been written by Mick Jagger and Keith Richards. Well, we'd have done it anyway – we had our own sound and our own approach to songs."

In *Life*, his 2010 autobiography, Keith Richards remembers that music-history fact too, but Keith is - of course - a bit more sardonic than Sir Cliff. In Chapter 5, the Glimmer Twin recounts the first unsteady steps on the songwriting path, a skill that Jagger and Richards only mastered after months of toil and "some terrible songs". Still, as Richards recalls with amazement, their manager managed to sell those "terrible songs" to other artists, who actually scored some minor hits with them:

> "We ended Cliff Richard's run of hits when he recorded our "Blue Turns to Grey"--it was one of the rare times one of his records went into the top thirty instead of the top ten. And when the Searchers did "Take It Or Leave It," it torpedoed them as well. Our songwriting had this other function of hobbling the opposition while we got paid for it. It had the opposite effect on Marianne Faithfull. It made her into a star with "As Tears Go By"-- the title changed by Andrew Oldham from the Casablanca song "As Time Goes By"--written on a twelve-string guitar. We thought, what a terrible piece of tripe. We came out and played it to Andrew, and he said, "It's a hit." We actually sold this stuff, and it actually made money. Mick and I were thinking, this is money for old rope!"

Keef has a particularly infectious, quite musical, narrative style. "Our songwriting had this other function of hobbling the opposition while we got paid for it" is a wonderfully assonant, almost poetic line, for example. But in terms of content, the Stone rather exaggerates. Cliff's "Blue Turns To Grey" is a No. 1 hit in Israel, scores second place in Malaysia and Singapore, reaches the

Top 20 in the Netherlands, New Zealand and Australia (when Dylan is in Australia), and in England it is also a neat No. 15 - in May '66, that is, when Dylan is in England. Cliff calling it "a hit" is in fact correct, and it certainly doesn't end his *run of hits* - the next four singles in this year 1966 all make the Top 10 again. Besides, Keith's salty qualifications like "this stuff" and "old rope" are really a bit too cynical; "Blue Turns To Grey" is actually a very nice song. And when the Stones record it themselves and Brian Jones brings in his twelve-string guitar, the nice song even gets a very charming, folk-rockin' Byrds colour.

However, the metaphor "blue turns to grey" remains somewhat awkward. After all, since the Middle Ages, "blue" has been the poetic, or synesthetic, synonym for "sad, depressed". So it is a bit confusing when Cliff and Mick Jagger sing:

> *So now that she is gone*
> *You won't be sad for long*
> *For maybe just an hour or just a moment*
> *Of the day*
>
> *Then blue turns to grey*
> *And try as you may*
> *You just don't feel good*
> *You don't feel alright*
> *And you know that you must find her*

... which communicates a confusing, incoherent message; the first stanza explicitly states that the narrator has been abandoned, and that he is therefore "sad" - he is *blue*. But that won't last long, and "then blue turns to grey". "Grey"? "Feeling grey" is, also according to researchers at the University Hospital South Manchester (2010) exactly the same as "feeling blue", only more accurate, more in line with the actual perception of depressed people:

"When asked to pick a hue that reflected their mood, healthy participants selected a shade of yellow, but depressed ones, for the most part, chose gray. According to the researchers, the color gray implies "a dark state of mind, a colorless and monotonous life, gloom, misery or a disinterest in life."

Dylan reuses the phrase in the penultimate verse of "Peggy Day", resolving the ambiguity in one fell swoop:

Peggy Day stole my poor heart away
Turned my skies to blue from gray
Love to spend the night with Peggy Day

... by the simple expedient of adding "*skies*" to the inverted metaphor. As it should be, of course. As Dylan remembers from such evergreens as "In a Little Spanish Town" (*Many skies have turned to grey / Because we're far apart*). And as it is done with appropriate melancholy by one of the most talented exponents of the 90s falsetto hype, by Travis in "The Last Laugh Of The Laughter";

When the spotlight fades away
Ma vie, c'est la vie
When the blue skies turn to grey
Ma vie, my oh my

Yep, my life was clouded and colourless, before I knew Peggy, and now the sun is shining, now my life is good. Pretty clear. Still not too uplifting poetry. Quite corny even. Which the master himself probably thinks too. "Peggy Day" is hardly a candidate, if a Martian came to Earth tomorrow and asked him: "Bob, how many iconic country songs have you made?"

V   What more can I say

A talent for self-mockery he had as well, Elvis. On the bootleg *I Sing All Kinds - The Nashville Sessions 1971*, there is an incomplete take of "Johnny B. Goode". When the final chord is fading away, Elvis suddenly starts again, now at half speed: "*I said... Johnny...*". Obediently, the obliging band picks it up right away, The King bursts into laughter and waves it away cheerfully, with a *just kidding*-undertone: "No, no, no, no". It is clear that the band has been conditioned to an "Elvis ending". Like the rest of the rock-loving world since 1956, for that matter.

It is the third track on Side 1 of the 1956 comet impact, the *Elvis Presley* album, the first rock and roll record to reach the top spot on Billboard, and the first rock and roll record to sell more than a million copies. The historical monument opens with "Blue Suede Shoes", followed by "I'm Counting On You", and then: "I Got A Woman".

Thanks to the moving "Bucklen tape", the earliest-known tape of Bob Dylan, recorded when he was around sixteen, we know that as a schoolboy Dylan was already starting to build his inner music encyclopaedia. In between rumbling through songs like "Jenny Take A Ride" and "Blue Moon", we hear young Robert Zimmerman chatting with his buddy John Bucklen;

> *Zimmerman*: You know they get all their songs, they get all their songs from little groups. They copy all the little groups. Same thing with Elvis Presley. Elvis Presley, who did he copy? He

> copied Clyde McPhatter, he copied Little Richard, ...
> *Bucklen*: Wait a minute, wait a minute!
> *Zimmerman*: ...he copied the Drifters
> *Bucklen*: Wait a minute, name, name, name four songs that Elvis Presley's copied from those, from those little groups.
> *Zimmerman*: He copied all the Richard songs.
> *Bucklen*: Like what?
> *Zimmerman*: "Rip It Up", "Long Tall Sally", "Ready Teddy", err ... what's the other one...
> *Bucklen*: "Money Honey"?
> *Zimmerman*: No, "Money Honey" he copied from Clyde McPhatter. He copied "I Was The One" - he copied that from the Coasters. He copied, ahhh, "I Got A Woman" from Ray Charles.
> *Bucklen*: Er, listen that song was written for him.

Young Zimmerman is largely right. "I Was The One" is not a Coasters song, but everything else is right. The choice of words is debatable, though. *"Copied"*, in particular, is a bit harsh. "I Got A Woman" is indeed a Ray Charles song, but Elvis does more than just copy; he makes the song his own, like in fact only Sinatra can make a song his own, and he does add something: at 2'08" we hear a closing bang, the song seems finished, but at 2'09" Elvis kicks in again, at half speed, for another twelve-second coda: the first "Elvis ending" is a fact.

The fans call it an "I Got A Woman-ending" as well, and that may be more accurate. Elvis recorded 767 songs, and only about ten to fourteen of them (depending on your definition) have such a dramatic coda at half speed. They are, however, spread throughout his career; "Got A Lot O' Livin' To Do" in '57 is the next one, in the '60s in about seven songs (including in the *68 Comeback Special* version of "Jailhouse Rock"), then in the ultimate kitsch "Winter Wonderland" (1971), and the last studio recording in which he applies this finale is "I Can Help" from '75. All in all, less than 2% of Elvis' recordings have an "Elvis ending", so to call it an "I Got A Woman-ending" is defensible. Moreover, "I Got A Woman" is indisputably one of the main pillars of his oeuvre. The man from Tupelo played it already in his Sun years (the recording is lost), it's the first song he recorded for RCA, and it was on the set list right up to his very last concert (Indianapolis 26 June 1977).

It is a bit of a mystery why Dylan chooses an Elvis ending in "Peggy Day" of all places. An open application? According to Dylan, Elvis is the greatest compliment his songs can receive:

> JW: Are there any particular artists that you like to see do your songs?
> BD: Yeah, Elvis Presley. I liked Elvis Presley... Elvis Presley recorded a song of mine. That's the one recording I treasure the most... It was called "Tomorrow Is A Long Time". I wrote it but never recorded it.

... that's what Dylan says in the *Rolling Stone* interview with Jann Wenner on 26 June 1969, four months after recording "Peggy Day". But Dylan must have acknowledged that "Peggy Day" is not Elvis-worthy. Without being able to define exactly what an "Elvis-worthy" song is, of course - but "Peggy Day" really isn't.

Maybe Dylan does it just to stretch the song a bit more, though. When he's finished, when the verses, twice the bridge and a repeat of the first verse have been completed, the clock only stands at 1'40" ... which would make it the second shortest song in Dylan's oeuvre, after "Father Of Night" (1'29"). Shorter still than "Oxford Town" on *The Freewheelin'*, which is a mere 1'50". With the Elvis ending from 1'41", Dylan stretches the tune another eighteen seconds, to 1'59", and then another 6 seconds of lead-out groove... final score 2'05". Longer now than "Oxford Town" and ex aequo with Dylan's third-shortest song, "The Wicked Messenger".

Elvis, despite the enticing finale, unsurprisingly ignores the song. But Dylan's Elvis dream still comes true again soon after: The King records "Don't Think Twice" in March '71, which will be released on the 1973 *Elvis* album. Making the song his own again, of course.

Dylan's bow to The King is elegant. When he himself adopts a country-rock approach to his live performances of "Don't Think Twice" in the 1990s, he is obviously reminded of his hero: he concludes the often long, drawn-out versions with an Elvis ending. Bloomington November '96, Atlantic City November '99, Cardiff September 2000... the Worcester '99 version is one of the longest, by the way - Dylan stretches the song to over seven minutes with a harmonica solo, and then throws in an Elvis ending of over half a minute.

"Don't Think Twice" has been performed more than 1100 times by Dylan. With and without an "I Got A Woman ending". "Peggy Day" has never been performed. That girl is out of sight.

7   Tell Me That It Isn't True

"I Heard It Through The Grapevine" is the first song of the legendary Motown duo Barrett Strong and Norman Whitfield and an indestructible classic right away. No chance hit either; they write dozens of songs, and among them there are quite a few monster hits and masterpieces. "Papa Was A Rolling Stone", "War (What Is It Good For)", "Just My Imagination", "Wherever I Lay My Hat (That's My Home)", just to name a few.

Initially, *Grapevine* is written for and in August '66 recorded by The Miracles, but only the third version, with Gladys Knight & The Pips (September '67), will be released on single and it reaches number two on the Billboard Chart. In the meantime, in the spring of 1967, Marvin Gaye records his now classic version for his breakthrough album *In The Groove*. Diskjockeys continue to run Gaye's album track and finally, in October '68, Motown decides to release that version as a single too. The song immediately rises to number one and stays there for nine weeks, until the end of January '69. It is Motown's biggest hit so far, scores high in the various All Time Best Songs lists and is inevitable in documentaries and films about the late 60s (although often the driven, drawn-out cover by Creedence Clearwater Revival is chosen).

When Dylan, in his hotel room at the Ramada Inn in February '69, quickly knocks together a couple of songs for the next recording day in Nashville, "I Heard It Through The Grapevine" still echoes through the streets, cafes and hotel lobbies. And with that, established Dylanologists such as Clinton Heylin and Tony Attwood argue, the inspiration for the undervalued "Tell Me That It Isn't True" has been explained.

Definitely thematically, but also in terms of content, the similarities seem undeniable. Just compare the opening lines of the world hit,

> *I bet you're wonderin' how I knew*
> *'Bout your plans to make me blue*

... to Dylan's words:

> *I have heard rumors all over town*
> *They say that you're planning to put me down*

... and the link is clear. Still, it is unlikely that *Grapevine* is the real source of inspiration - at best it is the trigger to the song that is much deeper in Dylan's genes, to the artist who is much closer to him, to Hank Williams' "You Win Again".

Dylan's admiration for Hank Williams is devout. In the autobiography *Chronicles*, he expresses his admiration for Luke the Drifter without restraint:

> "In time, I became aware that in Hank's recorded songs were the archetype rules of poetic songwriting. The architectural forms are like marble pillars and they had to be there. Even his words — all of his syllables are divided up so they make perfect mathematical sense. You can learn a lot about the structure of songwriting by listening to his records, and I listened to them a lot and had them internalized."

Alright, perhaps an all too sophisticated word choice, and that *forms like marble pillars* is not entirely coherent, but his meaning is clear: to Dylan, Hank Williams is a Great One, in terms of status comparable with Woody Guthrie and Elvis.

In the hundred episodes of his radio program *Theme Time Radio Hour* Hank is frequently played (eight times), never without obeisances: "One of the greatest songwriters who ever lived," TTRH 17, and: "Made some of the most beautiful songs about living in a world of pain," TTRH 7. And he loves to play them, too. From the *Basement Tapes Complete* we know Dylan's version of "Be Careful Of Stones That You Throw", the song Dylan learned from Hank Williams' alter ego Luke the Drifter, and of course "You Win Again".

"You Win Again" is a bitter country blues that Williams records one day after his divorce from Audrey Williams and expresses the betrayal that Hank feels. "The songs cut that day after Hank's divorce seem like pages torn from his diary," biographer Colin Escott says. And the opening words of this song resonate much more clearly than those of *Grapevine* in "Tell Me That It Is Not True":

> *The news is out, all over town*
> *That you've been seen, a-runnin' 'round*

His adulation of Hank Williams in *Chronicles* illustrates the impact of these words: "When he sang 'the news is out all over town,' I knew what news that was, even though I didn't know." And one line hereafter we see that Dylan is now making the same associative leap as in 1969: "I'd learn later that Hank had died in the backseat of a car on New Year's Day, kept my fingers crossed, *hoped it wasn't true.*"

In interviews from that time Dylan emphasizes that these songs, the songs on *Nashville Skyline*, come from within:

> "The songs reflect more of the inner me than the songs of the past. They're more to my base than, say *John Wesley Harding*. There I felt everyone expected me to be a poet so that's what I tried to be. But the smallest line in this new album means more to me than some of the songs on any of the previous albums I've made."
>
> (interview in March '69 with Hubert Saal for *Newsweek*)

And in the *Rolling Stone* interview with Jan Wenner that takes place in May, Dylan tells enough humbug ("When I stopped smoking my voice changed... So drastically, I couldn't believe it myself"), but credible is the statement that he arrives in Nashville with only a few songs in his pocket, and dashes off the other songs on the spot. Clinton Heylin, who is completely on the wrong track by supposing that "Tell Me That It Isn't True" is a parody of "I Heard It Through The Grapevine", analyses accurately again that the song belongs to the songs which, like a Basement Tape, in a short creative flash bubble up out of nowhere. Apart from Dylan's own words and the studio logs, the simplicity of the text also appears to support that assumption.

Indeed, there is no trace of *Blonde On Blonde*'s poetry, not an inch of *John Wesley Harding*'s depths. Clichés from the country idiom, rhymes like the ones that have been bouncing off these studio walls in Nashville thousands of times, although the poet seemingly deliberately, sometimes, turns to irony: *he's tall, dark and handsome* (it's not too realistic that a betrayed lover describes his rival as an irresistible Cary Grant).

Nevertheless, it is a beautiful, if not: *professional* song and it is not entirely understandable that its status has remained so far behind "I Threw It All Away" and "Tonight I'll Be Staying Here With You". The master himself also ignores the song for a long time; it takes thirty-one years, until March 2000, before he plays it on stage for the first time. But then Dylan actually seems to recognize the beauty of this old shelf warmer. "Tell Me That It Isn't True" will remain on the setlist until 2005 and is finally adequately rehabilitated after some eighty performances.

Satisfactory, but too late for an overall revaluation. The rest of the music world neglects this unsung Dylan pearl, so this work belongs to the rather select club Dylan songs of which hardly any covers have appeared. From Beck circulates a mediocre living room recording and he is the only artist from the Premier League that plays the song at all.

The Rosewood Thieves, folk rockers from New York, the indie rock band Kind Of Like Spitting (on *Professional Results*, 2014) and the remarkable Jolie Holland are worth mentioning from the lower echelons. Jolie Holland, who is rightly classified as *New Weird America*, is blessed with a smooth, drawling vocal style and repeats her idiosyncratic homage to Dylan on her album *Wildflower Blues* (2017); there she conjures up Dylan's forgotten "Minstrel Boy".

Just like Jolie Holland, Richard Janssen from Utrecht has a soft spot for Dylan's orphaned disposables. In 1998, for a so-called *2 Meter Session*, he records a beautiful "If Dogs Run Free". Ten years earlier, with his Fatal Flowers, one of the best Dutch bands of the 80s, he records the most beautiful cover of "Tell Me That It Isn't True", also for a *2 Meter Session* on VARA Radio. The Fatal Flowers are in the history books thanks to the very nice hit "Younger Days", but the other songs also stand the test of time well. The recording of "Tell Me That It Isn't True" is successful enough as to be selected in 2002 for the nostalgic collection album *Younger Days - The Definitive Fatal Flowers*.

He truly was tall, dark and handsome, our Richard Janssen.

8   Country Pie

I   People try and read so much into songs

In 1987, fanzine *Look Back* publishes in issue #15, "Fifteen Jugglers", a funny little interview with Dylan that a subscriber managed to score by pure coincidence. Reader Phil A. Roddy works at a fitness club in those days. He gets a call one Tuesday from his boss. If Phil could come and open the club the next day after closing time for an unnamed big shot who wants to do his workout in peace. This does occur, every once in a while, so Phil is not too surprised. He *is* when, much to his excitement, he lets *Bob Dylan* in the next night. He keeps his cool, well, up to a point anyway, and quietly observes how the then 45-year-old, muscular Dylan diligently and smoothly works hard for forty minutes on the various fitness machines. Afterwards, Dylan swims a few laps in the pool. When he then switches to the jacuzzi to relax, Phil gathers his courage, and, with tacit permission from the huge bodyguard, approaches Dylan. He confesses to being a fan and asks if he could do an interview for that fanzine *Look Back*. Dylan is relaxed, and allows it - on condition that Roddy doesn't record anything, and he has to join him in the jacuzzi. Phil happens – lucky coincidence no. 2 - to have mastered shorthand, quickly grabs a few sheets and a clipboard, takes off his clothes and slips in.

It is a charming but otherwise unexciting interview. "How often do you work out?" and whether he has ever had weight problems, that level. But the latter question does lead the conversation into a remarkable song analysis. Dylan explains that he ate almost nothing in the '65-'66s because of chronic toothache. But "when I had that motorbike accident, they did some root canal work for the next year and that took me out of pain I'd been in for two fucking years." Which is a not too well-known, rather startling biographical fact, but Phil seems to miss it. At least, his follow-up question is rather silly; "So, at that time you began to exercise?" Fortunately, Dylan is apparently in a talkative mood, and, unlike Phil, he does stay on track:

> "Not really, other than walking. I did one thing though. Man, did I eat. You name it. People try and read so much into songs. You know that song, *Country Pie*? That's what it was about. Pie. In fact, for the first time in six years, I began to have a bit of a weight problem."

Maybe Phil should have checked the calendar. Today is 1 April. And Dylan has a reputation, still in the 80s anyway, for having a penchant for talking complete nonsense with a perfectly straight face, April 1 or not. Still, it is quite surprising that this forgotten song in particular should bubble up in Dylan's mind. It is almost twenty years ago that he recorded the track in two takes on a Friday night in Nashville, and after that he never looked back at it - and after this ad hoc interview in 1987 it will be another thirteen years before "Country Pie" appears on his set list (10 March 2000 in Anaheim, and then the song's here to stay for a while: that year Dylan will perform "Country Pie" more than a hundred times).

More surprising though, is Dylan's song analysis (*"it's about pie"*). The introduction is undeniably true: "People try and read so much into songs." True, plenty of pompous bullshit has been written about this song, yes. Back when the album was released, it took Hubert Saal only five days to crack the code in *Newsweek* (14 April 1969). The chorus, with all those different pies, is "a kind of declaration of independence," Hubert explains. And:

> "When Dylan talks of eating pies, all kinds, he means writing songs, all kinds. And when he goes on in the song to say "Ain't runnin' any race" he seems to be rejecting the musical direction his many admirers have chosen for him in the past or would choose for him in the future."

Ridiculous enough, but at least kinder than Dylanologists like Mike Marqusee, Clinton Heylin ("embarrassing, un-Dylanesque drivel") or John Hughes ("almost provocative vapidity"), who qualify the song as a throwaway. Fans, meanwhile, overwhelmingly lean towards Dylan's own 1987 analysis, defending on the various forums opinions like "Bob Dylan basically just likes pie. I think we all do". Though among them are some who prefer to milk the double entendre *pie = vagina*, and even, believe it or not, analysts who can explain that *the song is about shooting heroin*.

Two camps, then, at two extremes of the spectrum; on the one hand, the lazy interpreters who deny the song any depth or ambiguity, on the other, the overenthusiastic cryptanalysts who even cite Shakespeare to prove the supposed scatological content of the lyrics. *Hamlet* Act 3, Scene 2 then, of course. The scene where Hamlet wants to put his head between Ophelia's legs. And assaults poor, dismayed Ophelia with doublespeak;

> *Ophelia*
>> No, my lord!
>
> *Hamlet*
>> I mean, my head upon your lap.
>
> *Ophelia*
>> Ay, my lord.
>
> *Hamlet*
>> Do you think I meant country matters?
>
> *Ophelia*
>> I think nothing, my lord.
>
> *Hamlet*
>> That's a fair thought to lie between maids' legs.
>
> *Ophelia*
>> What is, my lord?
>
> *Hamlet*
>> "Nothing."

... with "country" being pronounced emphatically as *cunt*-ry, and "*nothing*" being a common euphemism in Elizabethan times for the female pubic region ("no-thing", nudge nudge wink wink). And "pie" is established in twentieth-century America as a metaphor for vagina, so there you go, with your "*country pie*".

It does seem a bit laborious, but alright, yes indeed: once you are in that tunnel of sexual innuendo, the rest of the lyrics are a treasure trove of ambiguities and obscenities. A second argument for entering that tunnel is the song lyric's sky-high *Basement* couleur. One would be tempted to think that Dylan, leafing back through his notebook, has come across an old, unused lyric from the summer of 1967, a leftover pie as it were, a playful scribble from that summer in Woodstock with the guys from The Band in the basement of the Big Pink, carefree playing songs from the Good Old Days, shaking nonsensical songs out of his trouser leg, improvising little masterpieces out of thin air, and merrily shuffling and mixing folk, country and blues classics.

For that's exactly what we hear already in the opening couplet of "Country Pie"...

II Slap that drummer with a pie that smells

Just like old Saxophone Joe
When he's got the hogshead up on his toe
Oh me, oh my
Love that country pie

In 1978, in the interview with Jonathan Cott for Rolling Stone, he says much the same thing in much the same words: "Then I heard the Clancy Brothers and hung out with them – all of their drinking songs, their revolutionary and damsel-in-distress songs." Chapter 2, "The Lost Land", of the autobiography *Chronicles*, the chapter set in New York, still before his first record deal in 1961, repeats it pretty verbatim. "I got to be friends with Liam," Dylan writes affectionately there, "and began going after-hours to the White Horse Tavern on Hudson Street." An Irish bar, full of *guys from the old country*, and there's singing all night long. "Drinking songs, country ballads and rousing rebel songs that would lift the roof." The rebellion songs particularly touch him, he claims, and for another half-page, the autobiographer explains what would attract him to them.

But when we take stock at the end of the decade, the hard numbers and bare facts do reveal that it was mainly the drinking songs and country ballads that got under his skin. "Brennan On The Moor" becomes the blueprint for "Ramblin' Gamblin' Willie", Dylan turns "The Parting Glass" into "Restless Farewell", "The Leaving of Liverpool" is transformed into "Farewell", he uses, much to the displeasure of writer Dominic Behan "The Patriot Game" for "With God On Our Side", "Reilly's Daughter" comes along in "Seven Curses", and we could go on and on. "You're pals with the wild Irish rover and the wild colonial boy," as he will say in his Nobel Prize speech - Dylan has grabbed copiously from the repertoire of his pals, the wild Irish Clancy Brothers.

Apart from all those appropriations, he is just as happy to play the songs unedited and unaltered, preferably also á la Clancy Brothers. "Moonshiner", "The Old Triangle", "Come All Ye Fair and Tender Ladies "... "They influenced me tremendously," he tells Bono in 1984, Liam Clancy is "a phenomenal ballad singer." Indeed: "I never heard a singer as good as Liam ever. He was just the best ballad singer I'd ever heard in my life – still is, probably" (interview with David Hammond, *The Telegraph* 18, Winter 1984).

Liam's version of the old drinking song "Rosin The Bow" (or "Old Rosin The Beau", or "Ol' Roison The Beau" - even after the song's first publication in 1838, variants with different lyrics and titles continue to emerge) was then played by Dylan in 1967 in the Basement with the guys from The Band, and an echo of it descends in this opening chorus of "Country Pie";

> *When I'm dead and laid out on the counter,*
> *A voice you will hear from below,*
> *Saying send down a hogshead of whiskey to*
> *Drink with old Rosin the Bow.*

... that archaic "hogshead" (¼ tun, it's an old capacity measure for liquor, derived from the Old Dutch *oxhooft*), which is far too unusual to penetrate into a Dylan song by any other means. Quite possibly Dylan heard A.L. Lloyd's version "Rosin The Beau" on 1956's *English Drinking Songs*, but if so, the Clancy Brothers still made more of an impression; Dylan sings the exact same version that The Clancy Brothers sing with Tommy Makem on *Come Fill Your Glass With Us* (1959, the LP with "The Parting Glass" and "The Moonshiner") and again on *The First Hurrah!* (1964).

It is a second hint that "Country Pie" is baked up from leftovers from the Basement. The first was that revelation in that 1987 interview suggesting that Dylan wrote the song after he got rid of his toothache and could eat pie again, which must have taken place sometime in early 1967. And another hint is the name choice of the antagonist, "Saxophone Joe". A name that fits wrinkle-free between Silly Nelly from "Million Dollar Bash", Missus Henry, Tiny Montgomery, Skinny Moo and Half-Track Frank, Quinn the Eskimo, Minstrel Boy and Sunny Child the Overseer from "Joshua Gone Barbados", and all those other colourful birds of paradise hopping around down there in the basement under the Big Pink. Again, a theoretical possibility is that the walking music encyclopaedia Bob Dylan is winking at an obscure B-side by The Memphis Five from the 1940s, "Saxophone Joe", a run-of-the-mill novelty song with, at best, an antiquarian charm;

> *There's a boy you ought to know*
> *He's a boy named Saxophone Joe*
> *He goes bee-do-loo, bee-do-loo, bah-de-loo-doo-tweet*
> *That big old boy named Joe*

... but the nonsensical plot, "Gee, I'm fond of rural pastry - just like Joe was when a keg of whiskey fell on his foot", is a fourth, overarching clue to the suspicion that Dylan has unearthed an old Basement lyric here. After all, this has a tone and colour similar to the silliness in Basement gems like, say, "Yea! Heavy And A Bottle Of Bread" (*Now, pull that drummer out from behind that bottle, bring me my pipe, we're gonna shake it, slap that drummer with a pie that smells*), "Tiny Montgomery" (*Pick that drip and bake that dough, tell 'em all that Tiny says hello*) or "Lo And Behold!" (*Now, I come in on a Ferris wheel, an' boys, I sure was slick - I come in like a ton of bricks*).

Just three fairly random examples of insane mise-en-scenes. There can effortlessly twenty more of this calibre be found on *The Basement Tapes Complete* - settings and snapshots of bizarre scenes in which Dylan, without any profundity, winks at half-familiar movie scenes, quotes without any relevance from old folk, blues or country songs, and paraphrases offhand from the Bible, literature or The Oxford Dictionary of Proverbs. Like here in this first verse of "Country Pie", that is;

> - the opening line that seems to nod to Louis Jordan's no. 1 hit from 1946, the irresistible "Jack, You're Dead" (*Just like old man Mose*), with Ol' Louis Jordan playing the saxophone, by the way;
> - the eccentric borrowing of *hogshead* from a Clancy Brothers song;
> - and the alienating, weird plottwist *Love that country pie*, introduced with the equally alienating, übercorny *oh me oh my*

... yep, we're back at 2188 Stoll Road, West Saugerties, New York. Open the door, Homer.

III   I'm your wicked Uncle Ernie

Listen to the fiddler play
When he's playin' 'til the break of day
Oh me, oh my
Love that country pie

The interpreters who are so fond of assuming peasant obscenities in "Country Pie" are provided with ammunition from the second verse at the latest. It is 1969, and *"playin' 'til the break of day"* is by now well established as concealing language for "making love all night long". In the decades before the sixties, we could still sing "dance all night 'til the break of day" ("Sleepy Time Down South", Bill Monroe's "Uncle Pen") fairly safely, without ambiguity suspicions, or "we'll twist 'til the break of day" (Hank Ballard), or "party until the break of day" (Gene Pitney), or "cabaret until the break of day" ("Sleepy Time Gal"), and a hundred more variants, all of which sing of fairly harmless nocturnal, usually public entertainment.

Sexual charge enters - naturally - via the blues. At most, anyway, in the more clandestine blues is captured what should happen around the break of day. Ma Rainey sings as early as the 1920s, in "Ma Rainey's Black Bottom's Blues";

Early last morning 'bout the break of day
Grandpa told my grandma, I heard him say
Get up and show your old man your black bottom
I want to learn that dance

... which already doesn't leave too much to the imagination. Or like Lightnin' Slim's diction does give away what he means by *I want to boogie to the break of day* ("Just Made Twenty-One"), which The Allman Brothers also seem to understand (*Boogie 'til the break of dawn*, "Every Hungry Woman"), and even Pete Seeger sings along when Arlo Guthrie enriches the indestructible "Midnight Special", though basically a prison song, with a spicy extra verse;

> *Now here comes jumpin' Judy*
> *I'll tell you how I know*
> *You know, Judy brought jumpin'*
> *To the whole wide world*
> *She brought it in the morning*
> *Just about the break of day*
> *You know, if I ever get to jumpin'*
> *Oh Lord, I'll up and jump away*

... all of which Dylan knows, of course, when he sings *playin' 'til the break of day* in "Country Pie". After all, he sang rather unambiguously less than a record-side and a half ago, some 20 minutes earlier:

> *Lay lady lay*
> *Lay across my big brass bed*
> *Stay lady stay*
> *Stay with your man a while*
> *Until the break of day*
> *Let me see you make him smile*

Less traditional, then, is the euphemism that Dylan opts for the male lover. When, in their bawdy upgrade of the already-raunchy "Good Morning Little Schoolgirl", the Grateful Dead name a protagonist who dwells *til the break of day* with the little schoolgirl, it is a *chauffeur* who wants *to ride your little machine*. And otherwise, the lover at dawn is a *dancer*, a *stranger* or a *boogie-woogie boy from the Henry Swing Club* (Lightnin' Slim), a *rider* or a *midnight cowboy* - but a *fiddler* he actually never ever really is. Perhaps Keith Moon forever smeared the function designation, with his *Tommy* contribution "Fiddle About" (*I'm your wicked Uncle Ernie / I'm glad you won't see or hear me / As I fiddle about*), but "fiddling" has always had dubious connotations anyway. Why Dylan chose it is unknown, obviously, but if he did indeed write the lyrics in 1967 in the Basement, it must have been in the spur of the moment, without too much poetic consideration. Maybe this morning at the breakfast table "Wabash Cannonball" came by on the radio in the kitchen, and the poet rewrote the refrain *Listen to the jingle* into *Listen to the fiddler*, or the antique cowboy song "Midnight On The Water" buzzed through his head, with the opening words *Play me a fiddle tune, sing me a song*, or maybe Dylan is again just quoting; from the oldie "Silas Lee From Tennessee", that is.

Even before Phil Harris achieves immortality as the voice of Baloo the Bear in *Jungle Book*, Thomas O'Malley in *The Aristocats* ('70), and Little John in *Robin Hood* ('73), he has long made a name for himself with his 1950s monster hit, "The Thing" and the 1945 hit that is his signature song, "That's What I Like About The South". But Dylan may have been singing along with Harris' version of "Open The Door, Richard" - the song that will pop up as "Open The Door, Homer" in the Basement this week. (On a side note: Tex Williams' "Close The Door Richard (I Just Saw The Thing)" is a rather unique double-barrelled answer song to both of Phil Harris' hits.)

Anyway, in that same novelty song corner is Phil Harris's cartoonesque "Silas Lee From Tennessee" from 1949, in which we hear Dylan's imperative from this second verse pass by verbatim a couple of times;

> *The musics ready to begin*
> *So listen to the fiddler play*
> *Take that carpet off the floor*
> *Leave your shoes outside the door*
> *Come on do your dancing chore*

... without the slightest erotic allusion, of course - this is truly a violin player, a fiddler who enchants the whole crowd, from high to low, with his rousing fiddle playing:

> *Yes from Hollywood to Boston, Mass*
> *Throughout the land the upper class*
> *They're choosing partners for a jamboree*
> *And now at every swell affair*
> *Who's calling steps and fiddlin' there*
> *No-one but Silas Lee from Tennessee*

Unpretentious and harmless, just like the other candidates from Dylan's inner jukebox in which fiddling is performed; The Clancy Brothers' "Ballad Of St. Anne's Reel" (*There's magic in the fiddler's arm*), and Bill Monroe's "Uncle Pen" - although a dirty mind presumably knows how to detect ambiguities in its chorus:

> *Late in the evening about sundown*
> *High on the hill and above the town*
> *Uncle Pen played the fiddle, lord how it would ring*
> *You could hear it talk, you could hear it sing*

But then again – a violin-playing maverick is an archetype in Dylan's output. Einstein plays an electric violin on Desolation Row, the protagonist in "Early Roman Kings" commands *Bring down my fiddle*, in "Waitin' For You" it's a bit sombre (*The fiddler's arm has gone dead*), and with the most famous of all, the one from "Vision Of Johanna", we can go in any direction again, as it should be in a mercurial Dylan song;

> *The fiddler, he now steps to the road*
> *He writes ev'rything's been returned which was owed*
> *On the back of the fish truck that loads*
> *While my conscience explodes*

... a fiddler in whom we can read all sorts of things, but a tireless lover fiddling with the missus's country pie until dawn – no, that does seem a bit far-fetched.

IV Sugar and spice and all things nice

> *Raspberry, strawberry, lemon and lime*
> *What do I care?*
> *Blueberry, apple, cherry, pumpkin and plum*
> *Call me for dinner, honey, I'll be there*

John Cale meets Dennis Wilson and Gilbert O'Sullivan in Twin Peaks and they play Tubular Bells. Ponderous comparison, but it does perhaps remotely approach the layered beauty of John Grant's masterpiece *Queen Of Denmark*. Gordon Lightfoot is also in there somewhere. As are Jacques Brel and Abba. But that still would fall far short of the mark. The Czars' ex-frontman's first solo album is arguably the best record of 2010, and track 2, "I Wanna Go To Marz" (actually just: "Marz") is arguably the prettiest song of 2010, casually winking at the prettiest song of 1971, Bowie's "Life On Mars?". Grant's life story invites one to see in the candy-coated ode more and less disguised references to his unhappy childhood as a lonely gay in a narrow-minded religious family in Colorado, or, easier still, to understand the candy tsunami as metaphors for his disastrous alcohol and drug addictions. And this is how many commentators explain the song. Given the sometimes painful candour of other songs on *Queen Of Denmark* it is perfectly understandable, but in this particular case the background is actually more poetic and still a touch more down-to-earth, as Grant explains:

> "Marz was a sweet shop from my childhood. It's now empty and for sale. But I got to visit before hand, and the woman who served me as a child was still there. They still made all their own candies and ice cream. After it changed owners, I went back again and was given of the original menus. In the song, I list all the names of the sundaes, and drinks like Green River. The song is about the gateway back to childhood and innocence, when things haven't become complicated."
>
> (*The Brighton Magazine*, 22 January 2011)

Very prosaic then, in fact, the opening couplet - but this personal back-story provides a touching sheen that is more poetic than all the drug and other misery stories suspected by the critics and analytics;

> *Bittersweet strawberry marshmallow butterscotch*
> *Polar Bear cashew dixieland phosphate chocolate*
> *Lime tutti frutti special raspberry, leave it to me*
> *Three grace scotch lassie cherry smash lemon freeze*
>
> *I wanna go to Marz*
> *Where green rivers flow*
> *And your sweet sixteen is waiting for you after the show*
> *I wanna go to Marz*
> *We'll meet the gold dust twins tonight*
> *You'll get your heart's desire, I will meet you under the lights*

It has a naive, childlike poignancy, a nursery rhyme-like quality. Which we have been conditioned to since the nineteenth century, since *Sugar and spice and all things nice / That's what little girls are made of*. And infectiously revived in 1964 by Smokey Robinson, once jokingly classified by Dylan as a great poet, in "That's What Love Is Made Of".

Music-wise, the first bridge of "Country Pie" is a rather old-fashioned, classic bridge. Still, as is common in pop songs, after the second verse, but not, as is common in pop music, a bridge from the verse to the chorus. The bridge of "Country Pie" is the *B* in an *AABA* structure, i.e. a bridge from verse 2 to verse 3.

Lyrically, it has the charm of *sugar and spice* and John Grant's "Marz" - coincidentally with even the same flavours as in Grant's little masterpiece (*raspberry, strawberry, lemon and lime*). But for those interpreters who want to stick to a scabrous interpretation, for whom *pie = vagina*, it is far from naive and childlike; here, then, the randy protagonist sings of the joys of promiscuity. Sort of like Jan Kiepura's 1935 classic "Ob blond, ob braun, ich liebe alle Frau'n" (*Whether blond or brunette, I love all women*), of which the legendary Nina Hagen then makes, some forty years later, a next lesbian sultry, enlarging step, in "Auf'm Bahnhof Zoo" (*Ob blond ob schwarz ob braun / Ich liebe alle Frau'n*, 1978). And Waylon Jennings somewhere in between doing a witty variant in "Silver Ribbons" (on - what's in a name - *Nashville Rebel*, 1966), incidentally a weak song on a weak album, despite support from Chet Atkins and *Blonde On Blonde* veterans Charlie McCoy and Hargus "Pig" Robbins;

> *I can't recall my mother she left when I was two*
> *Brunets blondes and red heads were the only love I knew*
> *Don't ask me where I'm going don't ask me where I've been*
> *Those Silver Ribbons will take me there and back again*

And just as Dylan's narrator doesn't care either, apparently: *whether raspberry, strawberry, lemon or lime, I love all pies.*

Not a Dylan, all in all, singing with autobiographical candour his new life's happiness as a good family man with a lovely wife and children in the Catskills - which is what so many critics and analysts seem so keen to hear in the song, and in the album at all (Scaduto: "down-home country songs"). Marqusee disqualifies it as "deliberate banality". Heylin, who finds the song "embarrassing", like most professional Dylanologists. "Over the edge of corniness," writes *Bob Dylan Commentaries*. The *reddit* thread about the song swings back and forth between the supporters of the erotic interpretation and the innocents, who "think that it's a song about being with your true love and sitting down to a nourishing delicious meal," who find that it "evokes pure domestic bliss", it's "lightweight", a "lil' ditty", it has "such a happy vibe", "This is a song about pie" ... the innocents are, by the way, firmly in the majority.

At the same time, the innocents - miraculously, and without exception - ignore the vast majority of the lyrics, all those fragments of text that, with the best will in the world, do not fit a sweet ode to domestic happiness. One Saxophone Joe getting an archaic whiskey keg on his toes, some neurotic violinist fiddling all night long - it requires quite a bit of mental acrobatics to hear "being with your true love" or "domestic bliss" in it. Not to mention the subsequent verses...

V It's weird, man

Saddle me up my big white goose
Tie me on 'er and turn her loose
Oh me, oh my
Love that country pie

The second most famous goose rider of all time is probably Nils Holgersson, the hero of Selma Lagerlöf's irresistible 1906 children's book. But then again, he does not ride a *"big white goose"*. First, Nils himself is magically reduced to the size of Tom Thumb by an angry gnome, and the goose he subsequently mounts, Mårten, is anything but "big"; he is the smallest and youngest gander on the farm. No, for that *"big white goose"* we will have to go to the most famous goose rider of all, to the other side of the world.

The Hindu gods all have their own *vahana*, an animal of their own that is their companion and means of transport, usually blessed with supernatural qualities. Vishnu has his eagle, Bhairava a dog, and Lakshmi travels on her own owl. And the God-Creator himself, the Supreme Being who created all these animals, fish and birds, Brahma, chooses for himself a *big white goose* - because geese can separate water from milk. Brahma sees this as a metaphor for being able to distinguish fact from fiction, lie from truth - which makes the goose good company.

We could even, with some creative wishful thinking, find a source, or rather: an inspiration for this, for the identification of

Dylan's protagonist with Brahma. Hermann Hesse's *Siddharta* is obvious, and confidant Allen Ginsberg, too, is quite fascinated by Eastern wisdom and Hindu philosophy in these years, larding his poetry with Vishnu, Shiva and Brahma, Vedic mysticism and Sanskrit;

> *Parallels: in Montmartre Rousseau*
> *daubing or Rimbaud arriving,*
> *the raw Aether*
> *shines with Brahmanic cool moonshine*
> *aftertaste, midnight Nostalgia*

... he writes, for instance ("Pertussin", June 1968) - Brahma and his colleagues are regulars anyway in Ginsberg's oeuvre between, say, 1960 and 1970. But a third possible source of inspiration, though anecdotal, is even more likely.

Assuming that "Country Pie" is indeed a forgotten relic from the Basement, we could then date the lyrics around the Bauls Of Bengal's visit to Woodstock and to Big Pink, to Dylan, manager Grossman and the boys from The Band in the autumn of 1967. Dylan is said to be quite enamoured with the Bengali musicians, whom we also see standing next to him on the cover of *John Wesley Harding*. And that those itinerant storytellers have told Dylan why Sarasvatī is sitting on a swan, and that Suka, the parrot of the green god of lust and love Kamaveda, sometimes turns into four women - quite imaginable.

Images and stories to which Dylan is all too receptive; "Traditional music is based on hexagrams," an impassioned Dylan argues to Nat Hentoff for a *Playboy* interview in autumn 1965. "It comes about from legends, bibles, plagues, and it revolves around vegetables and death. There's nobody that's going to kill traditional music. All these songs about roses growing out of peoples brains and lovers who are really geese and swans that turn into angels - they're not going to die." He seems to mean it. Shortly before this outpouring he is equally inspired in another interview, the interview with Nora Ephron and Susan Edmiston for the *New York Post* (September '65), stating in much the same words:

> BD: Folk music is the only music where it isn't simple. It's weird, man, full of legend, myth, bible and ghosts. I've never written anything hard to understand, not in my head, anyway, and nothing as far out as some of the old songs. They were out of sight.
> E/E: Like what songs?
> BD: Little Brown Dog, "I bought a little brown dog, its face is all gray. Now I'm going to Turkey flying on my bottle." And Nottamun Town, that's like a herd of ghosts passing through on the way to Tangiers. Lord Edward, Barbara Allen, they're full of myth.

Dylan improvises on the spot a lyric variation on the ancient, frenzied "Little Brown Dog", which he probably learned about through Judy Collins (on *Golden Apples Of The Sun*, 1962):

> *I buyed me a little dog its color it was brown*
> *Taught him to whistle to sing and dance and run*
> *His legs they were fourteen yards long his ears they were broad*
> *Round the world in half a day on him I could ride*
> *Sing terry'o day*

... which Dylan himself will record as "Tattle O'Day" in March 1970, a year after "Country Pie", again with producer Bob Johnston. In which, by the way, he sticks to Judy Collins' version of the lyrics - frenzied enough by itself, so no Turkey bound flying bottles.

At the Basement, we have already been able to hear how much those "far out, out of sight" songs then feed his creativity. "Don't Ya Tell Henry", "The Mighty Quinn", "Yea! Heavy And A Bottle Of Bread"... songs with simple, catchy melodies, with word games and rhyme fun and above all: with exuberant tattle. Exactly, in short, what we hear here in "Country Pie", and very much so in this particular verse, in which the protagonist admittedly does not ride around the world on a little brown dog in half a day, in which no dove-luring Eskimos loiter by, no forty-nine bats linger under an apple suckling tree, and in which no herd of moose flies to Tennessee ("Lo And Behold") - but in which, at least as frenziedly, a protagonist does have his big white goose saddled, is tied on it rodeo-style, and will try to stay on when this big white goose is let loose.

A single tenacious Freudian might still manage to see veiled allusions to sexual intercourse even here, but then risks making himself a little ridiculous. After all, a scabrous interpretation implies comparing our poultry rider's female counterpart to a "big white goose". Any erotic expressiveness is thus definitely evaporated, unfortunately.

No, after Saxophone Joe and the toe-crushing *hogshead*, the nocturnal fiddler, the nine kinds of pie, and now this goose rider, we may finally say goodbye to both the - increasingly hard to follow – "domestic country song" proponents and the "bawdy pub ditty" subscribers. We truly are in the Basement. *It's weird, man, full of legend, myth, bible and ghosts.*

VI   "A clear statement of Dylan's present credo"

I don't need much and that ain't no lie
Ain't runnin' any race
Give to me my country pie
I won't throw it up in anybody's face

Rolling Stone reviewer Paul Nelson thinks *Nashville Skyline* "could well be what Dylan thinks it is, his best album," and writes a corresponding jubilant review, 31 May 1969. It's a particularly friendly song-by-song review, and Nelson thus also dwells on "Country Pie". And has an original opinion on the lyrics of this second bridge: *Ain't running any race/Get me my country pie* [sic]*/I won't throw it up in anybody's face* is "a clear statement of Dylan's present credo."

Leaving aside the naive premise that the first-person narrator in the song is Dylan himself, which besides by common sense should by now have been adequately disproved by Dylan's mantra, "credo" if you will, *je est un autre*, it is also puzzling what the reviewer considers a "clear statement". None of those three verse lines is unambiguous. In fact, the third, *I won't throw it up in anybody's face*, is downright puzzling. From the overall tenor of the review, it can be deduced that Nelson qualifies the LP as a testament to Dylan's "new-found happiness and maturity", and elevates to "credo" then the arguably weakest verse line of the entire album, *Love is all we need/It makes the world go round*, from the bridge of "I Threw It All Away" (which Nelson, as if to illustrate the facile superficiality of his article, after the rattling quote of the *give to me my country pie* line from this second middle eight, again misquotes; it's *Love is all there is*).

Content-wise, this second bridge falls a bit out of tune, here in "Country Pie". No eccentricities such as giant geese, marathon violinists, Saxophone Joe with his hogshead or a pie assortment, but still Basement-style bollocks. Only the opening line *I don't need much and that ain't no lie* is untainted by this, with Basementesque humour. But Basementesque nonetheless; after all, filler lyrics that Dylan plucks here and there from his vast working memory we also know from the Big Pink. Throwaways like "One For The Road" and "I'm Alright" consist entirely of rock and country clichés, and in gems like "Odds And Ends" or "This Wheel's Of Fire", the improvising song poet, as here in "Country Pie", glues up the gaps between the frenzies with whole and half quotes from the canon.

Curtis Mayfield & The Impressions, then, would be an educated guess. In Basement songs like "I'm Alright" and especially "All You Have To Do Is Dream", we have already heard more echoes of Curtis' best Chicago soul records of the 1960s, *People Get Ready* (1965) and *Keep On Pushing* (1964), the record we also see on the cover photo of *Bringing It All Back Home*. Robbie Robertson, especially, is a fan, judging by the many Curtis guitar licks he sneaks into Dylan's basement songs. And snippets of lyrics can be heard everywhere - like this *"I don't need much"*, from *People Get Ready*'s delightful opening track, the modest hit "Woman's Got Soul";

> *Now I'm just a regular fellow*
> *I don't need much*
> *I don't need a Cadillac car*
> *Or diamonds and such*
> *But the woman that I hold*
> *She's got to have soul*

Of course, *"I don't need much"* is far too generic to attribute to one unique source - but *if* "Country Pie" is a Basement relic, which seems more than likely by now, Curtis is an obvious candidate. Just as, say, Chuck Berry's "I Got To Find My Baby" (1960) can be designated as the obvious purveyor of the subsequent rock 'n' roll cliché *that ain't no lie* - especially since we hear as many Chuck Berry echoes as Curtis Mayfield fragments in those same Basement songs;

> *I got to find my baby*
> *I declare that ain't no lie*
> *I ain't had no real good loving*
> *Since that girl said goodbye*

Well, technically not a Chuck Berry song, actually. But "I Got To Find My Baby" or "Gotta Find My Baby", though written by Peter Clayton in 1941, is more or less confiscated by Berry - when The Beatles play the song (live at the BBC, 1963) they also seem to think they are covering a Chuck Berry song. With, incidentally, a splashy harmonica contribution by Lennon, which Dylan will also appreciate (although the 1956 version by the "King of the Harp" Little Walter probably is one step higher up in his gallery of honour).

Anyway, Dylan's *I don't need much and that ain't no lie* is the remarkably unremarkable stepping stone to the terzet that the *Rolling Stone* critic considers "a clear statement of Dylan's present credo", to *Ain't running any race/Give to me my country pie/I won't throw it up in anybody's face.*

That last line is of course the most striking, and especially for that peculiar "throw *up* in a face". No mistake; that's how it is published in the official *Lyrics*, and that's how we hear Dylan sing it in both the official release on *Nashville Skyline* and in "Take 2" on

The Bootleg Series 15 - Travelin' Thru (the outtake released on *The Bootleg Series 10 - Another Self Portrait* is cut short a few seconds before this passage of text). Weird; it's admittedly conceivable that a playful Dylan, a certified slapstick fan, would want to do something with *pie-in-the-face-throwing*. "Daydream", the 1965 Lovin' Spoonful hit from his mate John Sebastian, is still in the air (*A pie in your face for bein' a sleepy bulltoad*), and apart from that, *any* entertainer who has already sung thirteen pies, like Dylan at this point in "Country Pie", will start throwing them, preferably in faces. But it takes a particularly villainous kind of humour to infect such an innocuous classic with the ambiguous "throw up"... and in particular "throw up *in a face*" is of a student-like nastiness that is miles away from all the homeliness and family happiness that reviewers like Paul Nelson see in it - bizarrely enough.

VII I thought it was just a regular peach tree

Shake me up that old peach tree
Little Jack Horner's got nothin' on me
Oh me, oh my
Love that country pie

"I see you've found the Sacred Peach Tree of Heavenly Wisdom," says Master Oogway shortly before his demise, as he catches Po emo-eating. "Is that what this is? I'm so sorry," says an honestly startled Po with a mouth full of comfort food, full of peach that is, "I thought it was just a regular peach tree." Screenwriters Ethan

Reiff and Cyrus Voris have done their research, it seems; the peach tree, under which Master Oogway will leave this world moments later, dissolving in a cloud of peach blossom, symbolises immortality in China.

A peach tree, in short, is never just a peach tree - even in *Kung Fu Panda* (2008), it is a "Sacred Peach Tree of Heavenly Wisdom". It is a family film, so the peach here - obviously - has a family-friendly connotation. Safe and at the same time old-fashioned; in the Middle Ages, peaches symbolised the Trinity (because a peach is flesh, stone and germ), but from the Renaissance onwards at the latest, the metaphorical quality shifts to lust, love, female body parts or "woman" at all (because of the soft skin).

Dylan knows that too, of course, when he sings *"Shake me up that old peach tree"*. Peaches, and fruit anyway, have lost all innocence in twentieth-century songwriting. Thanks mainly to Bo Carter, the foremost ambassador of *dirty blues*, who alternates educational gems like "Pussy Cat Blues", "Please Warm My Wiener" and "My Pencil Won't Write No More" with fruity ambiguities like "Banana In Your Fruit Basket" or "Let Me Roll Your Lemon". And to a pioneer like Blind Lemon Jefferson, who starts filling the fruit basket with songs like "Peach Orchard Mama" (1929, *Peach orchard mama, you swore wasn't nobody gonna use your peaches but me*).

But at the time of the Basement, Dylan presumably was mainly singing along with Sonny Boy Williamson II, who also has "Peach Orchard Tree" in his repertoire, who sings "Until My Love Come Down", in which the harmonica master serves up a complete fruit cocktail;

> *I like yo' apple in your tree*
> *I'm crazy 'bout yo' peaches, too*
> *I'm crazy about your fruit, baby*
> *'Cause you know just how to do*

And otherwise with Yank Rachel's "Peach Tree Blues" from 1942, on which Sonny Boy plays along:

> *Don't them peaches look mellow, hanging way up in your tree*
> *Don't them peaches look mellow, hanging way up in your tree*
> *I like your peaches so well, they have taken effect on me*

... of which, incidentally, Big Joe Williams then makes "Don't Your Plums Look Mellow Hanging On Your Tree". But both variants owe their euphoniousness, of course, to the inspiration of others; to Kokomo Arnold's "Milk Cow Blues" (*Don't that sun look good, going down*, 1934) or to Leroy Carr's "Alabama Woman Blues" (*Don't the clouds look lonesome across the deep blue sea / Don't my gal look good when she's coming after me*, 1930), which Dylan lovingly copied on to "It Takes A Lot To Laugh, It Takes A Train To Cry".

The comrades in the Basement, The Band, experienced "the most magical day of our lives" (Levon Helm's autobiography *This Wheel's On Fire*, 1993) in the spring of '65 when they spent an afternoon spontaneously jamming with Sonny Boy in Helena, Arkansas, shortly before his death, so the line from Sonny Boy Williamson II to the Basement to Dylan's "Country Pie" is pretty short. Yielding, in all likelihood, Dylan's familiarisation with the association *peach tree = female body*.

But: Dylan is Dylan. So, unambiguous it seldom is, and a Dylan in Basement-mood most certainly isn't. Each dirty blues squares an ambiguity like *Shake me up that old peach tree* with a subsequent, equally piquant metaphor. "*Squeeze it the whole night long*", for instance, *"I'm gon' climb up on your top limb"* or *"You gotta give me some of it 'fore you give it all away"* or endless variations with grabbing, picking, shaking, snatching, or rattling and more obvious allusions to lovemaking. But hardly any dirty bluesman would have the nerve to follow up his *ding-a-ling*'s desire for *pie, peach, lemon, poodle* or *sugar bowl* with a children's verse like *"Little Jack Horner's got nothin' on me"*, so with an unequivocal reference to:

> *Little Jack Horner*
> *Sat in the corner,*
> *Eating his Christmas pie;*
> *He put in his thumb,*
> *And pulled out a plum,*
> *And said, "What a good boy am I!"*

... the eighteenth-century nursery rhyme in which an apparently not too savvy smug gobbler demonstrates utterly misplaced pride after performing a totally pointless act. Unknown in pop music, though, Little Jack is not. Shortly before *Nashville Skyline*, Stevie Wonder's "Do I Love Her" does occasionally pop up on the radio (*Bees love honey, banks love money / Birdies love to fly / Little Jack Horner in the corner loves his Christmas pie*), and in the Basement days, Dylan undoubtely is familiar with Skip & Flip's 1959 Top Twenty hit, the unpretentious sing-along "Cherry Pie";

> *Like Little Jack Horner sat, sat, sat in the corner*
> *Eating his cherry, cherry pie*
> *I didn't put in a thumb*
> *I didn't pull out a plum*
> *I guess I'm not as great as he, whoa-oh, whoa-oh*

... in which - coincidence, presumably - the associative leap from *cherry pie* to *country pie* is even smaller than the one from *Christmas pie* to *country pie*. But anyway, still closer under Dylan's skin is that one bluesman who has little hesitation about larding obscene allusions with quotes from nursery rhymes, one of the giants we've been hearing resonating in Dylan's oeuvre for sixty years now:

> *My sister's name is Puttentang,*
> *If you ask me again I'm gonna tell you the same,*
> *My brother's name is Little Jack Horner*
> *Mama told to watch the baby he didn't wanna.*
>
> *Putt told papa when he got home,*
> *Papa, papa, he sassed and moaned,*
> *Papa looked at brother with fire in his eyes,*
> *Brother started doin' the hand jive.*

... "Nursery Rhyme" from Bo Diddley's first LP with a funny cover, 1959's *Have Guitar Will Travel*. On the 1966 collection *The Originator*, the song is renamed "Puttentang" - the peculiar name seems an obvious mutilation of the French noun *putain*, but most online fans suspect a corruption of an alleged slang word for *vagina*, "pootang". Either way: slightly obscene. And the nod to Johnny Otis' "Willie And The Hand Jive" (1958) is less debatable, of course. On the other hand: *this* Jack Horner has the decency of refraining from poking his fingers in any pie. Or squeezing any peaches.

VIII   Nine words that changed my life

> *Ready or not here I come*
> *Gee that used to be such fun*
> *Apples peaches pumpkin pie*
> *Who's afraid to holler I?*

One of the many pleasant surprises of *The Basement Tapes* is the corny, churting parody of Bobbie Gentry's exceptional world hit "Ode To Billie Joe", which inspired Dylan's deliberately saltless throwaway "Clothes Line Saga". Although, throwaway... when 34 years later The Roches adorn the tribute album *A Nod To Bob* (2001) with their version, the raw lump of ore from the basement turns out to contain a shining jewel. By then, the three Irish-American sisters from New Jersey have had the song in their repertoire for more than 20 years, and that prolonged polishing, refining and sanding has by then taken the featherweight trifle into, as Dylan would say, the stratosphere, into the regions where only Very Great Dylan covers are allowed. Where Hendrix's "All Along The Watchtower" is, and Derek Trucks' "Down In The Flood", "Tangled Up In Blue" by the Indigo Girls, those regions.

Dylan's inspiration is not that hard to trace; in that same summer of 1967 when the men have their playtime in the basement, Gentry's "Study of Unconscious Cruelty" (her words) dominates the charts; the song is a mainstay on the radio. And the radio DJ digging into the Billboard Top 20 for his playlist in the late summer of '67 will, in many cases, snap up a neighbouring hit that accompanies "Ode To Billie Joe" in those same months: "Apples, Peaches, Pumpkin Pie" by Jay & the Techniques, a dated but still enjoyable soul stomp. A relaxed Dylan, relieved of his toothache and finally pie-eating again, listening to the radio in the background at the breakfast table in the morning, scribbling down a witty response to *Billie Joe* in his notebook, quickly writes "pie assortment" down in the margin – should yield some funny lyrics at a later point, the self-confident best songwriter in the world knows.

At least, that is an attractive scenario on the premise that the lyrics of "Country Pie" are a leftover from the Big Pink. Which does seem very likely, after all. Just as nice a guess would then be the scenario that an inspiration-seeking Dylan, a year and a half later in a motel room in Nashville, leafing back through his notebook, gets struck by *Saxophone Joe*, the pie assortment and especially the word "country".

We know that Dylan arrived in Nashville with only "a handful of songs", or, to be more precise: "The first time I went into the studio I had, I think, four songs" (*Rolling Stone* Interview with Jann Wenner, 1969), and that even the idea of making an album only surfaced after a day or so. And that "Tonight I'll Be Staying Here With You", the "Girl From The North Country" duet with Cash and "Nashville Skyline Rag" only emerged sometime after the first day of recording. It seems obvious then that Dylan arrived with the songs that were also recorded first: "To Be Alone With You", "I Threw It All Away", "One More Night" and "Lay, Lady, Lay". The only tune that follows "Lay, Lady, Lay" on that 13th February is the rather directionless, clearly improvised on the spot "Western Road" - it seems plausible that the basket was empty at that point, and that the rest of *Nashville Skyline*, including "Country Pie", was not written until after this 13th February.

It is even quite likely that a lot of the music and melody are only conceived on the spot, in the studio on February 14. Session musicians pianist Bob Wilson and guitarist Charlie Daniels, the two driving forces of "Country Pie" both emphasise the free, unstructured nature of the *Nashville Skyline* sessions. As Charlie puts it at the Letterman Show, 27 July 1982:

> "That was some of the freest… about as free as you can get in the studio, because he wanted you to do, you know, what you wanted to do. As opposed to somebody telling you exactly what to do. He would want you to put your own self into it, your own style of playing and all."

It is something they are not used to at all, and it is especially clear from the stories of the eternally grateful Charlie Daniels, that the musical accompaniment to songs like "Nashville Skyline Rag" and "Country Pie" came more or less out of the blue.

Charlie Daniels being eternally grateful, as he is convinced he owes his entire career to nine words spoken by Dylan during the *Nashville Skyline* sessions. He tells the story often, like here for the *Grammy Foundation Living History* interview in 2017:

> "They had a really good guitar player booked that had worked with him before, that was booked for all 15 sessions, but he couldn't make the very first one for some reason. He was booked on another session. And they asked me to come in and fill in for him, which I did, and I literally… I was playing guitar and I literally hung on everything that Dylan did, every chord he played, every note that came out of his mouth. I was sitting there looking at him and playing, and when the session was over, I was packing my gear up, I was fixing to leave, and Dylan asked Bob Johnston: where's he going, and he said he's leaving, I got another guitar player coming, and then Bob Dylan said nine words that changed my life. He said *I don't want another guitar player, I want him.*"

It is a story Daniels gladly retells, almost always in roughly the same words (including that dramatic "he said nine words that changed my life"). Explaining: Dylan "had a big enough heart that he put the name of the session players on the back of his album, pretty prominently actually," and that changes everything. Not only for his own self-confidence and status, but "it gave me a validity that I could have worked years and years to try to find."

Sympathetic and modest, but perhaps a little *too* modest; Charlie Daniels' exceptional talent would have taken him to the Premier League without Dylan's nine words just as well. Dylan sped it up a bit, probably. Moreover, Daniels - out of that same sympathetic modesty - underplays the reciprocity; that *Nashville Skyline* owes its charm and magic in no small part to Charlie Daniels. That is, anyway, what quite a lot of insiders with a right to speak argue...

IX   When Charlie was around, something good would usually come out

> "Country Pie" is a song that I played a guitar part on - my favourite guitar part ever played on a Dylan song, back on *Nashville Skyline*. I wanted to do it different, so I played fiddle on this. But it is just a good-time tune, you know. I think it's kinda Bob's concept of country life: "Give to me my country pie".
> (Charlie Daniels on his "Country Pie" cover on *Off The Grid*, 2014)

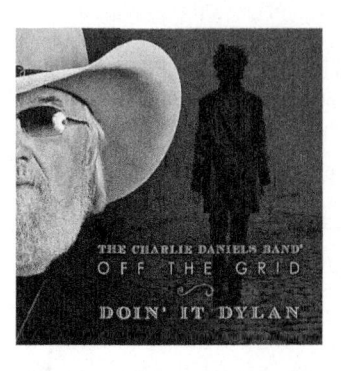

At the talk-show-style book launch of Ron Cornelius' book *The Guitar Behind Dylan & Cohen* at Nashville's Music Hall of Fame, 2017, Charlie Daniels and Bob Wilson sit next to each other on stage. So the conversation, despite Cornelius having absolutely no involvement in the album, a few times drifts off to *Nashville Skyline* - which is, after all, the album where Wilson and Daniels met, the breakthrough for Charlie Daniels, and the album that is at the intersection of Cornelius, Bob

Johnston, Dylan and both musicians. And to that joyous, frequent drifting off we owe insights and backstories about the origins of individual songs like "Country Pie" and the album at all. Recalling "Country Pie" in particular enthuses Daniels:

> "Something that always sticked in my mind with *Nashville Skyline* is when Bob started doing "Country Pie". And I had my Telecaster and Bob [*Wilson*] had the piano, and he started playing those chords and Bob started playing tadeladeda-tatataa... I never forget that, that's my favourite piano part you ever did, and then I came in on the Telecaster, remember that? [*singing:*] "And just like old Saxophone Joe when he got the hogshead..." and I just..., I mean..., it just blew..., we were just.., but that was the spirit of things I mean: we were having *fun*."

He stumbles over his own words, bursts out in infectious laughter almost 50 years after that evening at Columbia Studio A, seems to completely forget about the other guests, the presenter and the audience, here on this stage in Nashville, and has a reminiscing, intimate entre-nous with Bob Wilson - who does confirm his stories in full. And then just wants to have said publicly:

> "But for Charlie Daniels and that Telly of his, *Nashville Skyline* would not have been *Nashville Skyline*. I mean, this guy was perfect. You got all these talented god-gifted guitarists in Nashville, but he was perfect for that album."

They wave praise at each other rather effusively, but it doesn't get awkward; the recording of "Country Pie" illustrates and supports both the memories and analysis of both men. It is true, after all; the song is carried by Wilson's funky piano intro and the bouncy, pleasantly intrusive encouragement of Daniels' Telecaster. Dylan's objection at the time, "I don't want another guitar player, I want him", is quite understandable. And in his autobiography *Chronicles* (2014), Dylan reaffirms his appreciation, even confesses to feeling a kind of soul affinity, and moreover, suggests a kind of dependence on Charlie Daniels' input:

> "I was wondering who he [*Johnston*] was going to bring to the sessions this time and was hoping he'd bring Charlie Daniels. He'd brought Charlie before, but he'd failed to bring him a few times, too. [...] When Charlie was around, something good would usually come out of the sessions."

... in which, as an aside, that oddly passive "I was hoping he'd bring Charlie Daniels" also stands out. This is 1970. Dylan has long since been in the position of being able to dictate who he wants to play with - but still seems unaware that he could order Jimi Hendrix, Glenn Gould, Paul McCartney and Gene Krupa to the studio, so to speak.

Our cliché expectations of country & western it definitely does not meet, the intro by the duo Wilson & Daniels. Which is hardly surprising: Bob Wilson hails from Detroit and indeed has soul in his blood and in his fingers, having made a modest name for himself in the years before with piano contributions to the San Remo Quartet's instrumental soul-muzak and sweaty, funky, flopped soul stompers like "All Turned On" and "After Hours" - which we also hear back in that blues trifle "Western Road", the improvisation he, as an encore, set in after "Lay, Lady, Lay" last night, 13 February 1969.

How song-defining Wilson's intro is, the prog rock dinosaurs of The Nice demonstrate, with one of the first covers of "Country Pie", still in its 1969 birth year. Side A of their over-ambitious LP *Five Bridges* is devoted entirely to the rather pretentious "The Five Bridges Suite", but no less brave is Side B: rock symphonic arrangements with jazz-rock-like excursions on

Sibelius' "Karelia Suite" and Tchaikovksky's "Pathetique". And then, No.3 of Side B, a bizarre interpretation of Dylan's "Country Pie", larded with Bach's "Brandenburg Concerto No. 6". How successful that is, is debatable, but Keith Emerson is obviously an extremely talented craftsman, and accurately hits the bearing of "Country Pie": he builds his entire excerpt on Wilson's piano pattern from the intro.

In the studio, Charlie Daniels also immediately picks up on its funkiness - his pinched guitar licks and rousing lines are closer to Curtis Mayfield than to Chet Atkins. Looking back on it fifty years later with justifiable pride, he still finds: "My favourite guitar part ever played on a Dylan song." Can't be topped, he apparently thinks in 2014, when he records the song again for his Dylan album *Off The Grid: Doin' It Dylan*; he swaps the Telecaster for his violin. He could have skipped the song, of course, but the *"good-time tune"* is irresistible - Charlie has contributed to some 30 studio recordings of Dylan originals (apart from *Nashville Skyline*, also for *Self Portrait* and *New Morning*), but this is the only song on his tribute album to which he returns (the other nine covers are mostly from the 1963-1967 period).

Fun, and *good-time*, indeed - but the fiddle does not compensate for the loss of that energising, funky guitar part. Fairport Convention demonstrates as early as 1981 that Daniels should have stayed true to himself; Richard Thompson, an utterly adept and original guitarist himself, takes his hat off to Charlie's input and in broad strokes copies the part. In an otherwise rather perfect cover from which the funk and ragtime has virtually evaporated - promoting the song to a dynamic country rocker. Including a ferociously-disrespectful, anarchistic rockabilly coda.

Still, it is only one of the rare covers. The song does not become a classic. Dylan himself ignores the song as well, more than thirty years, until he suddenly resuscitates it in 2000, playing it over a hundred times. In rather faithful, funky and hoppy versions, with a starring role for Larry Campbell's solo guitar, usually playing attractive derivatives of Daniels' template. After 2001, "Country Pie" does pop up on the setlist a few more times, but after a final performance in 2007, it is over.

The latest revival for now comes from the good old Nitty Gritty Dirt Band, the guys who have been distinguishing themselves at times with fine Dylan covers since the 60s and crowned it in May 2022 with the very attractive tribute album *Dirt Does Dylan*. Beautiful cover design and filled with nice to very nice versions of everyman's friends like "She Belongs To Me", "Quinn The Eskimo", "Forever Young" and "Don't Think Twice". Plus one outsider: our half-forgotten country-funk gem "Country Pie". This time in a folky, unpretentious pub version.

Listen to the fiddler play.

Monday, February 17, 1969
2:00-5:00 pm

Studio A
Columbia Recording Studios
Nashville, Tennessee

Produced by Bob Johnston

Take 1 - 2
Nashville Skyline Rag

Take 3 - 13
Tonight I'll Be Staying Here With You

Take 14 - 24
One Too Many Mornings

Take 25 – 31
I Still Miss Someone (*Johnny Cash/Roy Cash jr.*)

Take 32 – 34
Don't Think Twice, It's All Right/Understand Your Man

Musicians:
Charlie McCoy (bass), Robert S. Wilson (piano), Norman L. Blake (guitar), Charlie E. Daniels (guitar), Pete Drake (steel guitar), Kenneth Buttrey (drums), and Hargus Robbins (piano). Johnny Cash (shared vocals).

9   Nashville Skyline Rag

I   "Do what you want to do"

"Nashville Skyline Rag," Jann Wenner asks in the 1969 *Rolling Stone* interview, "was that a jam that took place in a studio or did you write the lyrics before?". Which is a bit of a difficult question. After all, the song has no lyrics. Dylan is polite enough not to correct him: "Umm.... I had that little melody quite a while before I recorded it." Still, Wenner's curiosity is nonetheless not misplaced and in fact understandable; "Nashville Skyline Rag" *does* sound as if it was mainly improvised on the spot. Plus: Dylan has never released an instrumental song on record before; indeed, something is a bit odd about the song.

Civilised, likeable, a little awkward, intelligent and prone to well-dosed pinches of self-mockery, plus some mild irony at times - the image that rises from interviews with "Spider" John Koerner over the decades is pretty constant. Totally in line with this is also the answer he gives when asked for his opinion on all those particularly nice things Dylan says about him in *Chronicles*:

> "Well, I've read the book," says John, "and sometimes what I see is either he's got a better memory than I have or he's making stuff up. It could be either way. Because some of that I don't remember all that well, but it doesn't mean it didn't happen. But the general sense of it is correct."
> (fRoots 325, July 2010)

... with which Koerner very civilly hints that Dylan is not too particular about factual matters. Incidentally, this will not so much concern the passages in which the autobiographer comments on his old friend's character and appearance: "Koerner was tall and thin with a look of perpetual amusement on his face. We hit it off right away. When he spoke he was soft spoken, but when he sang he became a field holler shouter. Koerner was an exciting singer, and we began playing a lot together." But presumably Koerner's surprise concerns, among other things, the songs he is said to have played to the young Dylan. "I learned a lot of songs off Koerner," Dylan writes;

> John played "Casey Jones," "Golden Vanity" — he played a lot of ragtime style stuff, things like "Dallas Rag."

Koerner does have a huge repertoire, that much is true. Both solo, and with Dylan's mate Tony Glover, and as a member of the legendary trio Koerner, Ray & Glover, he recorded dozens of songs, all of which we find again on Dylan's set and track list. Either one-on-one or re-worked or paraphrased. "Delia", "Froggie Went A-Courtin'", "When First Unto This Country", "The Days of '49", "St. James Infirmary", "Danville Girl", "Corrina"... and that's just a fraction of the songs whose echoes we hear back with Dylan. *I learned a lot of songs off Koerner* doesn't seem to be an overstatement. But that "Dallas Rag" was among them is unlikely - Koerner never recorded that song and it is not on any of his setlists. On guitar, it is played by men like Stefan Grossman and Mark Knopfler (with his charming occasional band The Notting Hillbillies, 1990) - a catchy performance really does require a technical skill slightly above the level of a good, but not towering guitarist like Koerner, in any case.

Though well within the capabilities of guitarist Norman Blake, one of the most illustrious pillars of Nashville Skyline's beauty.

By 1969, Norman Blake has long made his mark at the top of rootsy country, bluegrass and blues, has been playing with Johnny Cash for years, and has everything that appeals to Dylan in these days: a deep love for traditionals, an encyclopaedic knowledge of the oeuvre of greats like Bill Monroe, Roy Acuff and The Carter family, and enviable skills on guitar, mandolin, dobro and fiddle. *And* an expressed, deep love for ragtime. Which is how it began for him, in his youth in the 1940s, as he explains to *The Bluegrass Situation* interviewer in February 2017:

> "Sam McGee was playing guitar. He was on there. He was playing solo-type guitar, playing with his brother Kirk. So I heard him."
> *Sam McGee? I've never heard of Sam McGee.*
> "You've never heard of Sam McGee!"
> *Well ... [laughs] I've heard of a good number of guitar players from back then, I think, but I don't know of him.*
> "Well, the McGee brothers. Sam and Kirk McGee. The Boys from Sunny Tennessee, they were billed. They played with Uncle Dave Macon. Sam played a lot with Uncle Dave, made records with him, and then he and his brother Kirk also made records. And then they played with Fiddlin' Arthur Smith, band called The Dixieliners."
> *What was his guitar style like?*
> "Sam was a finger-style guitar player, played guitar-banjo and played guitar, kind of a ragtime style. They were extremely good, some of my favourite people. I used to hear them on the Opry when I was a kid."

After his interlude with Dylan, Blake remains at the top. He is a regular in Johnny Cash's band, helps Joan Baez to a hit with his contribution to "The Night They Drove Old Dixie Down", plays dobro on the Nitty Gritty Dirt Band's best-selling *Will The Circle Be Unbroken*, wins Grammys, including one for his contribution to the *O Brother Where Art Thou* soundtrack (2000, Norman plays "You Are My Sunshine", "Little Sadie" the instrumental version of "I Am A Man Of Constant Sorrow", and "Big Rock Candy Mountain"), is a sound-determining member of John Hartford's band and thus one of the founders of the so-called *newgrass* sound (*Aereo-Plain*, 1971), and ragtime remains a constant in Blake's repertoire from his first solo album (*Home in Sulphur Springs*, 1972) to setlists deep into the 21st century.

The recording sessions for that landmark Newgrass record by John Hartford must have given Norman Blake a sense of déjà vu. "John let us play what we wanted to play. 'Cause that's one of the beautiful parts about it-he just let us get in there and pick," says colleague Tut Taylor in the John Hartford essay in Ray Robertson's *Lives of the Poets (with Guitars)*, 2016, about working on *Aereo-Plain*. Exactly the same as what Blake experienced two years earlier with Bob Johnston and Dylan, as we know thanks to the Letterman interview with Charlie Daniels ("he wanted you to do what you wanted to do").

The fruits of that freedom are effortlessly traceable: on *Aereo-Plain*, we hear Blake going all-out on side two, in "Symphony Hall Rag", and no doubt we owe "Nashville Skyline Rag" to that same freedom. A year after the *Nashville Skyline* sessions the song is on John Hartford's setlist, along with Norman Blake live (*Turn Your Radio On,* 1971), where Hartford introduces "Nashville Skyline Rag":

> "Uhmm, let's see... I guess we should introduce Norman Blake next. I guess I can best introduce him by saying that people who read their liner notes closely, will know who he is. He plays on a lot of sessions. With people such as Johnny Cash and Joan Baez and Bob Dylan... I guess that's one of my favorite Dylan albums, *Nashville Skyline*. Plays the definitive version on that."

And again a year later Blake showcases the roots of "Nashville Skyline Rag" on his debut album, in "Richland Avenue Rag" - all recordings that demonstrate what happens when Bob Dylan gathers top country musicians around him on a Monday afternoon in Nashville, and then says: "These are the chords. This is the melody. Do what you want to do."

II   Some of the names just didn't seem to fit

On 9 April 2019, the trustees of the Al Clayton Photography estate post on social media the photo that graces the back cover of *Nashville Skyline*. With explanatory text:

> "50 years ago today the Nashville Skyline album was released. Al shot the back cover. Story: Al had heard Dylan wanted a certain "look" for the back cover. We have recently discovered all of the slides he shot while searching for "the" image. [...]. When Al saw this one, he went to Johnny Cash's home. There was a party going on. Dylan was there. Al walked up and placed this picture on the table and asked "Is this what you're looking for?" The rest is history."

Interesting enough, but it still leaves plenty of question marks. Clayton selects one of his photographs, in the apparent belief that this is "the certain look" Dylan is looking for - the famous photo with the Nashville skyline. Which suggests that Clayton already knew the album's title. Which in turn suggests that the album was named after the song "Nashville Skyline Rag" (and not the other way around). Dylan's own statements about the title choice don't clarify much either, but they do clarify something. In the lengthy 1969 *Rolling Stone* interview, Jann Wenner explicitly asks about it, shortly after Dylan reveals that an initial title was *John Wesley Harding, Volume II*, and that the record company wanted to call the LP *Love Is All There Is*. Which is killed by Dylan with the enigmatic, self-contradictory argument "I didn't see anything wrong with it, but it sounded a little spooky to me." Yes, but where then *did* the final title *Nashville Skyline* come from, Wenner wants to know;

> "Well, I always like to tie the name of the album in with some song. Or if not some song, some kind of general feeling. I think that just about fit because it was less in the way, and less specific than any of the other ones there. Certainly couldn't call the album *Lay Lady Lay*. I wouldn't have wanted to call it that, although that name was brought up. It didn't get my vote, but it was brought up. Peggy Day – *Lay Peggy Day*, that was brought up. A lot of things were brought up. *Tonight I'll Be Staying Here With Peggy Day*. That's another one. Some of the names just didn't seem to fit. *Girl From The North Country*. That was another title which didn't really seem to fit. Picture me on the front holding a guitar and *Girl From The North Country* printed on top. [*laughs*] *Tell Me That It Isn't Peggy Day*. I don't know who thought of that one."

It does seem as if Dylan is just making something up on the spot. At least, it seems very unlikely that all those Peggy Day variations were actually serious proposals. The first part of his answer, though, "I always like to tie the name of the album in with some song. Or if not some song, some kind of general feeling", sounds very plausible. After the corniness of the trite, embarrassing album title *Another Side Of Bob Dylan*, so from *Bringing It All Back Home* onwards, Dylan reserves the right to name his own LPs. And indeed, the four albums since then do express a "general feeling", or are "tied in with some song", and in half the cases both at the same time (*Highway 61 Revisited* and *John Wesley Harding*). Just as *Nashville Skyline* both is "tied in with a song" and expressing a "general feeling".

Fine choice of title, then. Which Dylan unfortunately undercuts a bit himself with the continuation of his motivation: "It was less in the way" - more or less dismissing the motivation for choosing *Nashville Skyline* as: the least bad of even worse options. Incidentally, he is of course right to disqualify candidate album titles like *Lay Peggy Day* or *Girl From The North Country* as "awkward, in the way". But surely *Nashville Skyline* is an excellent, apt, original title. Better at least than other extremes like *Planet Waves* and *Empire Burlesque*, to name just two - after all, Dylan misses as often as he hits the mark, with his album titles.

The most likely scenario, all things considered, is that on Monday afternoon, 17 February 1969, producer Johnston asks: "What do you want to call it?" after recording the instrumental they had just improvised. He needs some title for the recording sheet. The inimitable Norman Blake just turned those few chords and "that little melody" into a splashy rag. "Nashville Rag?" Dylan tries, not too imaginatively. "Already exists," ragtime expert Norman Blake will presumably object (and he's right; "Nashville Rag" was written by legendary female ragtime pioneer Mamie Gunn back in 1899).

"Just make it Nashville Skyline Rag then," says Dylan, after taking a quick glance outside, meanwhile trying to think of how the chords of the next song, "Tonight I'll Be Staying Here With You", went.

III   The long-haired hippies and their drugs

The Soggy Bottom Boys they call themselves, the unlikely folk sensation that breaks through like a bolt from the blue with "Man Of Constant Sorrow", in the Coen Brothers' enchanting love project, *O Brother, Where Art Thou* (2000). A band name, which, like many names and scenes in the film, kindly nods to a cultural phenomenon from twentieth-century America, in this case to the Foggy Mountain Boys, the backing band of legendary bluegrass duo Flatt & Scruggs.

Dylan is a passive but still destructive force in the duo's career. After 20 highly successful years, during which traditionalist Lester Flatt's resistance to his mate Earl Scruggs' drive for experimentation and innovation continues to erode, something inside of Flatts dies, presumably during the recording of their last record together, 1968's *Nashville Airplane*. Scruggs and producer Johnston push through four Dylan covers: bluegrass versions of "Like A Rolling Stone", "I'll Be Your Baby Tonight", "The Times They Are A-Changin'" and even "Rainy Day Women #12 & 35". Meanwhile, the places of the former-familiar Foggy Mountain Boys have been taken by men who have just recorded *Blonde On Blonde* and *John Wesley Harding* with Dylan, or will be heard shortly afterwards on *Nashville Skyline* and *Self Portrait*: Charlie Daniels, Bobby Moore, Henry Strzelecki and Kenny Buttrey. And in the producer's chair these days is Dylan producer Bob Johnston. None of which Lester likes. In *Bluegrass: A History* (1985), the standard work by the eminently knowledgeable professor Neil V. Rosenberg, Flatt's uneasiness is catchily, though not academically, articulated:

> "Behind the scenes, Lester Flatt was very dissatisfied with their material; he didn't like singing Bob Dylan and was disgusted by the long-haired hippies and their drugs. He refused to perform the new songs, and this became a source of contention between him and the Scruggses."

... and the professor knows very well what he is talking about. In the liner notes of the compilation album *Flatt & Scruggs* (1982), he already incorporated excerpts from interviews with Flatt:

> Lester Flatt felt uneasy with Bob Johnston: "He also cuts Bob Dylan and we would record what he would come up with, regardless of whether I liked it or not. I can't sing Bob Dylan stuff, I mean. Columbia has got Bob Dylan, why did they want me?"

Scrolling back through the discography, however, we have to hand it to Lester: he has demonstrated a respectable amount of tolerance, he did put up with it for quite some time. From May 1966 to the last recordings with Earl in August 1969 (i.e. well after the release of *Nashville Airplane*, the recording sessions forming the second-to-last drop), he bowed his head no less than *nineteen* times, playing yet another one of those damn Dylan hippie songs. "Honey, Just Allow Me One More Chance" is, ironically, the very last one. Released on the album that hit the shops after the irreparable break-up, as a kind of *Let It Be*: the aptly titled 1970's *Final Fling - One Last Time (Just For Kicks)*. With even more indirect Dylan input; SEVEN Dylan covers. And Dylan's unofficial bandleader in Nashville, Supreme Nashville Cat Charlie McCoy, joined too (harmonica). It's almost beginning to look like poor Lester Flatts was, in fact, bullied out.

You can kind of hear it too, with hindsight. From Lester's vocals on "Girl From The North Country", "Wanted Man", "One Too Many Mornings" and "One More Night" drips dejection, some fatigue and reluctance, and only "Maggie's Farm" seems to be able to light a flame. And, well alright, in the announcement of "Nashville Skyline Rag", understandably the only Dylan song Lester really likes, we can actually hear a trace of enthusiasm:

> Lester: "Earl, what's the name of this tune"?
> Earl: "The Nashville Skyline Rag."

Earl, however, has long been a full-blooded Dylan fan. Which is also well illustrated in the 1972 documentary *The Bluegrass Legend - Family & Friends*. The recordings in that living room with Dylan and with Earl's sons Gary and Randy are weirdly moving - not so much because of the music, which is fine, but because of the moments around it, because of the interaction of Dylan and Scruggs;

> "Have you heard this latest version of your song *Nashville Skyline Rag*?" the meek Earl Scruggs asks, smiling shyly
> "Yeah," Dylan replies, appearing equally bashful.
> "Could... could we just try that one?"
> "Okay."

Touching. As is Earl's half proud, half acknowledgement-seeking smile after the final chord.

The actually somewhat silly (by Dylan standards anyway) "Nashville Skyline Rag" remains quite popular with the peers -

especially in country and bluegrass circles, of course. And surely this will be mostly due to the missionary work of giant Earl Scruggs. With Scruggs, the song remains on the repertoire, in his Earl Scruggs Revue, the band with his sons in which Dylan songs at all remain a regular part of the setlist - the live album *Live! From Austin City Limits* from 1977 opens again with the *Rag*, for instance.

Banks & Shane (1975), J.D. Crowe & The New South (1976), Knoxville Grass (1977), Knoxville Grass (1978)... meanwhile, the next generation of bluegrass, alt-country , cowpunk and all its variants, long-haired potheads or not, keep "Nashville Skyline Rag" alive with recordings and live performances as if passing on a relay baton. Even into the generation after that; in the twenty-first century, it's the children's children, bands like Monroe Crossing, The Abrams Brothers and the David Grier Band, so that the song seems to be gradually becoming a kind of rite of passage; apparently, it belongs on your setlist if you want to count yourself in bluegrass circles.

None of them add anything to the original. At most if the band happens not to have a banjo or mandolin, it sounds a nuance different (like Dan Whitaker & The Shinebenders, 2006), but otherwise the dozens of covers in the twenty-first century are all equally enjoyable and utterly interchangeable. Which is perfectly fine, of course.

10   Tonight I'll Be Staying Here With You

I   To have and have not

In 2004, out of 22,838 entries from 111 countries, *Habseligkeiten* is chosen as "German word of the year". The jury, which included singer/songwriter Herbert Grönemeyer and author Uwe Timm, state that they are touched by the "friendly, pitying undertone", and at the same time it makes the owner of *Habseligkeiten* seem "sympathetic and lovable".

It indeed *is* a wonderful word. It means more than just "possessions". Lexically, it connects two areas of life: earthly possessions (*haben*, "to have, to possess") and bliss (*Seligkeit*, "bliss, benediction") that is unattainable in earthly life. This tension leads the reader to have positive feelings towards the owner of the *Habseligkeiten*. The love for the small, in itself perhaps worthless things is understood as a "condition for happiness".

"*In der Beschränkung zeigt sich erst der Meister*, only in confinement the master reveals himself", Goethe asserts, as if to explain why he is making things so difficult for himself, in the 1780s. The by then long world-famous poet escapes his degeneration into a magistrate and the stifling court life in Weimar, takes a sabbatical of three years in Italy (1786-88) and returns born again: back to the Antiques it shall be. With all the restrictions that entails: stripped-down tragedies without scenery, a minimum of action, hardly any supporting actors and endless monologues in Alexandrian lines. Tightly drawn poetry within strictly defined frameworks of fixed rhythm and rhyme. Retellings of material that has existed for centuries (*Iphigenia in Tauris*, for instance).

Within all these limitations, Goethe says, it takes mastery to be able to move and captivate. And, sure enough, there is something to be said for that. We admire The A-Team, getting locked up in an old shed once again, and then managing to construct a bazooka with the devastating power of a hydrogen bomb only using *objets trouvés* like rubber bands, rusty drawing pins and chicken wire. Or the unworldly surgeon who performs life-saving emergency surgery on the floor of the airport departure lounge with the help of a straw, a pocketknife and a biro - *in der Beschränkung zeigt sich der Meister*.

The genesis of the tight, minimalist masterpiece "Tonight I'll Be Staying Here With You" gives no reason to think that its creation was a deliberate attempt to create a masterpiece within self-imposed limitations. But the rigid frameworks within which Dylan squeezes the song do suggest it.

On Wednesday 12 February 1969, Dylan arrives in Nashville with only half an album of songs in his suitcase. The rest for *Nashville Skyline* will be either written on the spot or improvised (such as the opening track, "Girl From The North Country" in duet with Johnny Cash). In June, when Jann Wenner interviews him for *Rolling Stone*, Dylan says:

> "The first time I went into the studio I had, I think, four songs. I pulled that instrumental one out… I needed some songs with an instrumental… Then Johnny came in and did a song with me. Then I wrote one in the motel… Then pretty soon the whole album started fillin' in together and we had an album."

The album, for which Dylan is still considering the title *John Wesley Harding Vol. 2*, is missing a closing track like "I'll Be Your Baby Tonight", et voilà: over the weekend, Dylan shakes a song out of his sleeve. Which is then recorded after the instrumental album filler "Nashville Skyline Rag" on Monday 17 February, when the working week has started again.

That song, *"one I wrote in the motel"*, must be "Tonight I'll Be Staying Here With You", which provides a fascinating glimpse into Dylan's working methods. Apparently, the world's best songwriter with performance pressure feels comfortable in a tight corset. He chooses quintins in an unusual rhyme scheme: *ABCCB*. It's somewhat archaic - an 11th-century archetype of the limerick has such a scheme, William Wordsworth uses it for "The Idiot Boy" (1798), and it provides a somewhat nursery rhyme-like playfulness - but actually Dylan just uses the same rhyme scheme he chose for "I Threw It All Away":

> *I once held her in my arms*
> *She said she would always stay*
> *But I was cruel*
> *I treated her like a fool*
> *I threw it all away*

… which he recorded the day before yesterday. In terms of content, obviously, diametrically the opposite of "I Threw It All Away"; the narrator in "Tonight I'll Be Staying Here With You" is on the other side of a love's affair time-line, is still in the very early stage of embracing his happiness of love unconditionally:

Throw my ticket out the window
Throw my suitcase out there, too
Throw my troubles out the door
I don't need them anymore
'Cause tonight I'll be staying here with you

Apart from that remarkable rhyme scheme, the cast-iron, again somewhat old-fashioned metre catches the ear: all verse lines work towards the refrain line with a four-foot trochee (DUM da DUM da DUM da DUM da), with a *trochaic tetrameter*, as the schoolmaster would say. Not necessarily very uncommon in the art of song, but unusual nonetheless. And very classical. Beethoven's Ninth for instance ("Ode To Joy", *Freude schöner Götterfunken*). Wordsworth's "Song Of Hiawatha", the Weird Sisters in *MacBeth* ("Fair is foul, and foul is fair / Hover through the fog and filthy air").

And, again, nursery rhymes. Dr. Seuss' *One Fish Two Fish Red Fish Blue Fish*. "Peter Pumpkin Eater" is perhaps the best-known shortcut to identify a trochaic tetrameter (*Peter Peter pumpkin eater / Had a wife and couldn't keep her*). And a work that keeps popping up in Dylan's output, William Blake's "The Tyger" (*Tyger! Tyger! burning bright / In the forests of the night*).

Attractive, and indeed not very common. The trochee simply clashes with our "natural" sense of rhythm, our sense of language that automatically steers us towards iambic rhythm structures. This may also explain the seemingly lazy opening, the somewhat easy choice to start three times with "*throw my ... out*". Still, a Goethe would have imposed a limitation like this on himself to demonstrate mastery in the continuation of those restrictive opening words. In which Dylan also succeeds, by the surprising turn from symbolic, but concrete possessions (*ticket* and *suitcase*) to immaterial inner stirrings, to the *troubles* that also go out the door. *Habseligkeiten*.

II Slut wives cheating

> *I should have left this town this morning*
> *But it was more than I could do*
> *Oh, your love comes on so strong*
> *And I've waited all day long*
> *For tonight when I'll be staying here with you*

Baby Driver (2017) is an entertaining action film, lovingly spiced up with unobtrusive details like leading colours, lighting, superior camera use, sound effects and especially, less unobtrusively: music. Protagonist Miles 'Baby' (Ansel Elgort), a very young, exceptionally gifted getaway driver, suffers from tinnitus and suppresses the whistling beeping almost continuously with music - a not too far-fetched alibi for director Wright to inventively synchronise the overflowing soundtrack's songs with storyline and action scenes. And for the Dutch viewers, there are two sequences that appeal to perhaps petty, but understandable national pride.

One is the brilliantly edited chase scene in which Baby escapes his assailants on the stop-and-go pattern, the rhythm and even the drum beats of Focus' 1973 world hit, "Hocus Pocus". The other Dutch hurrah moment is Golden Earring's "Radar Love" (1973), which is considered an alternative Dutch national anthem anyway. And, as with the actual national anthem, no one knows the correct lyrics. Especially the third verse has the most bizarre phonetic abberations, but officially it should be:

> *The radio's playin' some forgotten song*
> *Brenda Lee's "Coming On Strong"*
> *The road has got me hypnotized*
> *And I'm speedin' into a new sunrise*

The final line is reworded as, for instance, *spitting into a nude sunrise*, but *Brenda Lee* causes the most problems. *Randal Lee, Brandon's lead, The melody's, Steadily, Reveille's, Randy Leeds, Brad and Lee are coming on home*... poor Brenda Lee has been overgrown by a thicket of wild onomatopoeic imitations. Not really blameworthy, to be fair - in the Netherlands, Brenda Lee has nowhere near the status and name that she has in the UK and the US, and "Coming On Strong" is completely unknown. An informed Dutchman knows at most "I'm Sorry" from 1960. But then, Golden Earring's singer and songwriter Barry Hay has a Scottish father, was born in India and attended an English boarding school in The Hague - Barry is a bit more international than the average Hollander. Plus: the band has just completed their first tour of America in 1969. A forgotten song like "Coming On Strong" might very well have been played on the radio there - perhaps also when Dylan, in his hotel room in Nashville, plucks "Tonight I'll Be Staying Here With You" from the air.

It seems a rather thin line, the line from "Coming On Strong" to *Oh, your love comes on so strong*. Still, the line becomes already a little thicker when we look not at Brenda Lee, but at the discography of the Queen Of Nashville, at Kitty Wells. It seems that Dylan has her 1967 *Love Makes The World Go Around* on the turntable these days. The title track is quoted verbatim in "I Threw It All Away";

> *Love is all there is, it makes the world go 'round*
> *Love and only love, it can't be denied*

... the song in which in any case echo more songs from the Kitty Wells album ("The Hurtin's All Over", "There Goes My Everything"). And the final song of the album is Kitty's version of "Coming On Strong" - again a lament of the abandoned love partner. "All the songs coming out of the studios then were about slut wives cheating on their husbands or vice versa," as Dylan says in *Chronicles* about Nashville (Chapter 3 "New Morning") - a concept Dylan also succumbs to once, here on *Nashville Skyline*, in the underrated gem "Tell Me That It Isn't True".

Wells' ultimate contribution to the cheating slut wife and ditto husband genre is also on *Love Makes The World Go Around*:

> *Straighten up your tie and comb your hair*
> *Look as though you spent your time alone*
> *Wash away her lipstick from your collar*
> *Get your lie the way you want it then come on home*

... "Get Your Lie The Way You Want It", the closing track of Side A. In terms of content and theme, it is the opposite of "Tonight I'll Be Staying Here With You", but stylistically it is a copy: just like Dylan's song, it opens with an accumulation of imperatives, of short commands from the first person to the love partner.

The album's appeal to Dylan is palpable. The album cover does not mention names of session musicians, but one Nashville Cat who also excels on *John Wesley Harding* and *Nashville Skyline* is not too hard to spot: Pete Drake's steel guitar dominates half of the songs. In the backing choir we recognise Elvis' favourite men, The Jordanaires, the unknown duet partner in heartbreaking songs like "The Hurting's All Over" provides an irresistible Everly Brothers sheen, and tremolo guitar like in "Once" must have taken Dylan back to magical moments from his youth, earth-shattering moments like the first time he heard "Uncloudy Day" by The Staple Singers. The song that shifts a not insignificant part of American rock music history, by the way. John Fogerty honours the monument too, in his autobiography (*Fortunate Son*, 2015):

> "The Staple Singers, "Uncloudy Day." The sound of that guitar—God, what a cool thing. That vibrato: *bewoowowow*. Even as a kid I could identify that sound right away. Pops Staples was doing all that. I loved that sound."

Dylan expresses his admiration somewhat more poetically, of course:

> "It was the most mysterious thing I'd ever heard. It was like the fog rolling in. I heard it again, maybe the next night, and its mystery had even deepened. What was that? How do you make that? It just went through me like my body was invisible. What is that? A tremolo guitar? What's a tremolo guitar? I had no idea, I'd never seen one. And what kind of clapping is that? And that singer is pulling things out of my soul that I never knew were there. After hearing "Uncloudy Day" for the second time, I don't think I could even sleep that night."
>
> (*AARP The Magazine* interview, 2015)

An inconspicuous footnote in Kitty Wells' rich discography, *Love Makes The World Go Around*. Filled with forgotten songs. But still coming on strong.

III   ... and cheating husbands

Dylan is quite firm, in the interview he gives to John Cohen and Happy Traum in the summer of 1968, to give the ailing folk music magazine *Sing Out!* a financial boost: "The song has to be of a certain quality for me to sing and put on a record. One aspect it would have to have is that it didn't repeat itself. I shy away from those songs which repeat phrases, bars and verses, bridges..." Actually, Dylan says, he wanted to record a whole album of other peoples songs, but "about nine-tenths of all the contemporary material being written" has those damned *repeating phrases* and *bridges*, so he went back to writing his own songs. Songs like "The Ballad Of Frankie Lee And Judas Priest" and "All Along The Watchtower", so we don't have to be too sad about Dylan's alleged dislike of choruses and bridges.

Fortunately, the bard is not too principled either. For his most recent album, *John Wesley Harding*, which is the thread of the conversation, he already plucked "I'll Be Your Baby Tonight" from the motel room air of the Ramada Inn in Nashville - a beautiful song which repeats phrases, bars and verses, and a bridge it has as well. It is not a one-off slip-up, not a rule-confirming exception. Six months after his declaration of principle, Dylan wholeheartedly embraces all those artifacts he so resolutely rejected; "To Be Alone With You", "I Threw It All Away", "Peggy Day", "One More Night", "Tell Me That It Isn't True", "Country Pie"... almost every song on *Nashville Skyline* repeats phrases, bars and verses, and has a bridge too. And in "Tonight I'll Be Staying Here With You" he doesn't "shy away from" a bridge either:

> *Is it really any wonder*
> *The love that a stranger might receive*
> *You cast your spell and I went under*
> *I find it so difficult to leave*

Textually, a hotchpotch of clichés. Mostly from recent radio hits, it seems. *Is it any wonder* Dylan has been hearing since he first played Hank Williams' records ("Kaw-Liga", for instance), and he hears the words every week on the radio. "So Sad" by The Everly Brothers, Ella Fitzgerald's "Walking In The Sunshine", "I'm In The Mood For Love", "Gentleman Friend", Cliff Richards' "I Only

Came To Say Goodbye"... the list is endless. Apparently we find it a nice word combination to sing. Equally chewed out and indestructible are all the word combinations with *under your spell*. "Don't Blame Me", for one, and everyone from Sinatra to Buck Owens and from "Black Magic Woman" to The Everly Brothers. And especially "I Put A Spell On You", obviously. And the third pillar under the bridge also is a third grab in the goldie-oldie box: the combination *love-stranger* is just as stereotypical as *any wonder* and as *under a spell*. One of the Four Tops' greatest hits, for example. "Shake Me, Wake Me (When It's Over)" still sounds often enough on the radio these days and can be found in any jukebox:

> *They say "She don't love him, she don't love him"*
> *They say my heart's in danger*
> *'Cause you're leaving me*
> *For the love of a stranger*

In terms of content the middle-eight builds, as befits a classic middle-eight, a bridge to a better understanding. Though it seems to completely elude analysts like Clinton Heylin (who understands a "message of reassurance"), Robert Shelton ("commitment to a love") and Michael Gray ("a deliberate announcement of the fall from restlessness") that the first-person narrator is an utterly unstable, emotion-driven rolling stone. The critics seem to be fueled by biographical facts, by their knowledge of Dylan's recent domestic, rural status as a young, newlywed father who has said goodbye to the frenzy of rock star life. Conveniently, they assume, as do annoyingly many Dylanologists, that the "I" is Dylan himself, and they also don't appear to look much further than the title to conclude that *I, Dylan*, is here wording his farewell to the restless feeling. And expresses a moving pledge of allegiance to his dear wife Sara, something like that.

Both Heylin and Shelton and Gray write this in the twenty-first century, when Dylan has been saying, in variants, for nearly fifty years now: *je est un autre*. The "I" in my songs is not "I, Bob Dylan". In vain, though.

In the bridge, the lyricist quite unambiguously confirms what was already suggested in the previous lines: the first-person narrator is not a loving husband bidding farewell to his troubled life, but rather a stranger passing by, following an impulse. He doesn't belong in this town at all, was already on his way to the station with his suitcase, probably heading home, but falls *under the spell* of some village beauty. Impulsively, he decides not to return to his troubles, he decides to throw away his train ticket and to stay the night with this irresistible lady. Granted, imperatives like "Throw my ticket out the window" can with a little tolerance be interpreted metaphorically, as poetic expressions of a desire to say goodbye to the hectic life of a restless rock star. But verses like "I should have left this town this morning" and "The love that a stranger might receive" do not fit into such a pliable interpretation - it really would take some surreal acrobatics to interpret them as romantic family man rhetoric. No, these are really the words of a cheating debaucher about to indulge in a one-night stand.

Dylan is in a motel in Nashville, after all. The classic décor of an extramarital escapade. In the town where "all the songs coming out of the studios then were about slut wives cheating on their husbands or vice versa."

IV   The cadence of click-clack

I can hear that whistle blowin'
I see that stationmaster, too
If there's a poor boy on the street
Then let him have my seat
'Cause tonight I'll be staying here with you

It would be going way too far to call Udo Lindenberg the German Bob Dylan, but still. His status, for starters, is quite comparable. Roughly speaking, Udo has since the beginning of the twenty-first century the same stature in Germany as Dylan has in the rest of the world since the beginning of the twenty-first century: respected in all corners of cultural circles, beyond criticism, living legend. The old rocker (he was born in 1946) also has been in the front trenches for half a century now, shaking up the German music scene with his *Panik Orchester*, is an accomplished painter (his works hang in museums and even in the *Bundeskanzleramt*, the German Chancellery), he writes books and since five decades, right up until 2021, his records are topping the charts.

More relevant similarities between Dylan and Lindenbergs are superior sense of rhyme and rhythm, respect for tradition, the infectious enjoyment of playing with language and the demonstrable influence on colleagues. A sublime example is "Sonderzug nach Pankow" from 1983, one of Udo's biggest hits.

Entschuldigen Sie, ist das der Sonderzug nach Pankow?
Ich muss mal eben dahin, mal eben nach Ost-Berlin
Ich muss da was klären, mit eurem Oberindianer
Ich bin ein Jodeltalent, und ich will da spielen mit 'ner Band

Pardon me Sir, is this the Special Train to Pankow?
I have to get over there, over to East Berlin.
I gotta sort something out with your Chief Indian.
I'm a yodelling talent, and I wanna play there with a band.

... Lindenberg actually tried for years to be allowed to perform in East Germany, and this song really was an attempt to get permission from "the Chief Indian", from Secretary General Erich Honecker. Tone and word choice, however, are absolutely melodious and funny, but not very diplomatic. *"Ey Honni, I sing for little money,"* for example, and further on Udo states that Honecker secretly, in the men's room, listens to rock 'n' roll on *West-radio*.

The template is Glenn Miller's immortal "Chattanooga Choo Choo" (1941), the first gold record in music history. Lindenberg picks up the opening words ("Pardon me boy, is that the Chattanooga Choo Choo?") transforms the *shoeshine boy* into a *stationmaster* and then takes the lyrics his inimitable way. *And the song starts, just like "Chattanooga Choo Choo", with a train whistle blowin'*.

It is one of the strongest and most popular images in a hundred years of song history: *the train whistle blowin'*. With the abolition of the steam whistle and the introduction of the air horn, it has actually become an archaic concept, but like *dial a number* or the floppy disk icon for "save", it is firmly anchored in our cultural baggage. Even in the twenty-first century, artists such as Kid Rock ("Cowboy"), The Tragically Hip ("Are You Ready") and Cake ("The Distance") still sing with straight faces about *lonesome whistles* that they could have never heard themselves.

Dylan's anchor points are easy to point out. There are dozens of records in his record cabinet on which a steam whistle is blowing anyway. "How Long Blues" by Dinah Washington, Conway Twitty 's "Mama Tried", "Southbound Train" by Big Bill Broonzy, "On the Atchison, Topeka And The Santa Fe", "I've Been Working On The Railroad", "Won't Be Long", "500 Miles"... without steam whistles, Dylan's record cabinet would be pretty empty. He'd even be missing his own first album:

> I got the freight train blues
> Oh Lord mama, I got them in the bottom of my rambling shoes
> And when the whistle blows, I gotta go baby, don't you know
> Well, it looks like I'm never gonna lose the freight train blues

... not to mention the song that was on his repertoire even before his first album, and which he performed on Cynthia Gooding's radio show, March '62:

> I was riding number nine
> Heading south from Caroline
> I heard that lonesome whistle blow
> Got in trouble had to roam
> Left my gal and left my home
> I heard that lonesome whistle blow

... Hank Williams' "Lonesome Whistle Blues", a heavy anchor under Dylan's oeuvre. And the other anchors are whistleblowers too. The second anchor is Harold Arlen's "Blues In The Night", the song of which almost every line recurs in Dylan's oeuvre.

"Blues In The Night", like "Chattanooga Choo Choo", was written in 1941, like "Chattanooga Choo Choo" for a movie, and both are nominated for the Academy Award for Best Original Song in 1942. And both lost, inexplicably, to Jerome Kern's "The Last Time I Saw Paris". Incomprehensible, because that is *a)* a pretty mediocre song, and *b)* not even an Original Song (the song is five years old by then). Jerome Kern, who hadn't even come to the awards ceremony, fully convinced that both "Blues In The Night" and "Chattanooga Choo Choo" were far superior to his "The Last Time I Saw Paris", felt so embarrassed that he personally made sure that the rules were tightened: from 1943, an Original Song must really be an Original Song, written especially for the film.

Too late for Arlen, of course. But still. "The Last Time I Saw Paris" was one of the few songs that year that did *not* involve the blowing of a steam whistle - perhaps that won over the Oscar jury. And "Blues In The Night" has reached its place of honour on the Olympus easily, even without that Oscar - not only because there are at least eight Dylan songs in which the song descends;

> *Now the rain's a-fallin'*
> *Hear the train a-callin, "whoo-ee!"*
> *My mama done tol' me*
> *Hear that lonesome whistle blowin' 'cross the trestle, "whoo-ee!"*
> *My mama done tol' me*
> *A-whooee-ah-whooee ol' clickety-clack's*
> *A-echoin' back th' blues in the night*

... nine, if we include "Tonight I'll Be Staying Here With You".

And the third, and heaviest steam whistle blower in Dylan's backpack is of course Johnny Cash. If only for Johnny's alpha and omega song "Folsom Prison Blues",

> *Well, if they freed me from this prison*
> *If that railroad train was mine*
> *I bet I'd move it on a little*
> *Farther down the line*
> *Far from Folsom Prison*
> *That's where I want to stay*
> *And I'd let that lonesome whistle*
> *Blow my blues away*

... and because of that whole earth-shattering debut album *Johnny Cash with His Hot and Blue Guitar!* (1957) too, the album with "The Rock Island Line" and Hank Williams' "I Heard That Lonesome Whistle" and "I Walk The Line" and "Doin' My Time" and "The Wreck of the Old '97"... the songs that make Dylan sigh in his autobiography *Chronicles*: "Ten thousand years of culture fell from him," and

> "The coolness of conscious obvious strength, full tilt and vibrant with danger. *I keep a close watch on this heart of mine*. Indeed. I must have recited those lines to myself a million times. Johnny's voice was so big, it made the world grow small, unusually low pitched — dark and booming, and he had the right band to match him, the rippling rhythm and cadence of click-clack. Words that were the rule of law and backed by the power of God."

... songs with words about prisoners with ball and chain, about John Henry, about Jesus and about tramps. And especially about trains. Lots of trains, all of them with *lonesome whistles*. As in "Train Of Love", the song Dylan picks for his contribution to the wonderful tribute album *Kindred Spirits* (1999).

Der Udo eventually managed to take his Special Train to Pankow after all. Eight months after the release of "Sonderzug nach Pankow", four years after his first request, Lindenberg is suddenly allowed to perform at the Palace of the Republic in East Berlin (25 October 1983). On condition that he does not perform "Sonderzug nach Pankow". The GDR leadership keeps him on a leash with the promise of a tour in 1984, but this promise is (of course) withdrawn after the *Pankow*-less concert. Three years after the fall of the Wall, in 1992, Leipzig fans paint the words *Sonderzug nach Pankow* on a train that does indeed travel to Berlin, and on 25 March 2015, thirty-two years after the release of "Sonderzug nach Pankow",

Lindenberg finally really does travel, by underground *U-Bahn* train, from West Berlin to the Far East, to Pankow. The *Oberindianer*, meanwhile, has long since become little more than an embarrassing memory from a bizarre past.

V Hits of sorts

The song has a somewhat peculiar hopscotch career. Dylan writes it quickly on a February weekend to fill up *Nashville Skyline*, it is recorded on Monday, and that's that. In August, at the Isle Of Wight concert, it's not on the setlist - the twin sister of "Tonight I'll Be Staying Here With You", the closing song of the previous *John Wesley Harding* record, "I'll be Your Baby Tonight", is preferred. Dylan does not perform any concerts in 1970 or 1971, but remarkably, he now considers "Tonight I'll Be Staying Here With You" a Greatest Hit; the song is selected for the successful *Greatest Hits Vol. 2*.

Collaborator and confidant Happy Traum, who assisted Dylan in recording "Down In The Flood", "You Ain't Going Nowhere", "I Shall Be Released" and the outtake "Only a Hobo" in September '71 especially for the compilation, reveals to Clinton Heylin a selection criterion for the songs: "He felt there were some songs that he had written that had become hits of sorts for other people, that he didn't actually perform himself, and he wanted to fit those on the record as well."

Traum is of course referring to the four songs to which he himself contributed, but it seems likely that the same considerations were made for the rest of the track list. After all, songs like "The Mighty Quinn" (Manfred Mann), "All I Really Want To Do" (Cher) and "All Along The Watchtower" (Jimi Hendrix), to name but three examples, were never hits for Dylan either, but rather *"hits of sorts for other people"*.

"Tonight I'll Be Staying Here With You", however, can hardly be called *a hit of sorts*. And all too often the song has not been covered either at that time, September 1971.

Cher is the first. For her underrated *3614 Jackson Highway* (1969) she records a soulful, brilliant version. Cher acts fast, by the way. Two weeks after the release of *Nashville Skyline.* And she also records the *Skyline* songs "Lay, Lady, Lay" (as "Lay, *Baby*, Lay"; even tough lady Cher prefers to avoid homoerotic connotations) and "I Threw It All Away" for this beautiful album, produced by Jerry Wexler in Muscle Shoals - equally great renditions, sounding even better on the 2000 remaster.

But it's not a hit - not even a single. About the same time, in May '69, Esther Phillips records her version. Just as soulful, and even more beautifully sung. This one is released as a single, but does not make any waves. Phillips uses the recording again a few months later, in October '69, as a B-side for the modest hit "Too Late To Worry, Too Blue To Cry" (#121 Billboard, #35 on the R&B charts). So Dylan has seen some royalties from it. And Esther's version seems to have some staying power as well; in 2010, 41 years after the recording, her cover is selected for the wonderful compilation *How Many Roads: Black America Sings Dylan*.

Not a hit either, but blessed with curiosity value and an irresistible dated sheen, is the single by British psychedelic rockers Orange Bicycle, again from 1969 (release 18 July). Orange Bicycle were a charming band that tried to ride along on the psychedelic wave, crafting attractive, Byrds-like songs to go with it. Their "Tonight I'll Be Staying Here With You" is in fact a bit of an outlier in their output (the B-side, "Last Cloud Home" is actually nicer), but at the very least it has a nostalgic quality, fifty years later.

The same applies, approximately, to the last pre-*Greatest Hits Vol. II* cover, legendary Ben E. King's funky jam session from 1970. Fuzzy guitars, James Brown vibe, soaring Hammond organ and even a gospel-like diminuendo... it is, in short, 1970 - with all its charm and all its clichés.

All in all, none of the covers deserves the qualification *hits of sorts for other people*. But nevertheless, the song gets the honour of being selected for the double album *Greatest Hits Vol. II* compilation. As the closing track of Side 2, the same side that opens with her twin sister "I'll Be Your Baby Tonight". And thus displacing hits like "With God On Our Side" and "If You Gotta Go, Go Now" (both a hit for Manfred Mann), and popular, much-covered songs like "Girl From The North Country", "Boots Of Spanish Leather" and "Love Minus Zero/No Limit"... to name just a few titles of songs that actually *do* deserve the qualification "hits of sorts". So it does appear as if "Tonight I'll Be Staying Here With You" has some special place in Dylan's heart.

The appearance is deceptive, as appearances usually are. The first concert after the *Greatest Hits* release (17 November 1971) is two years and two months later, the first concert of the 1974 Tour of America with The Band on 3 January in Chicago. The setlist is dominated by crowd pleasers, Dylan playing plenty of songs from the first and second Greatest Hits compilations, but no "Tonight I'll Be Staying Here With You". Notwithstanding the fact that the song's status has only grown in the meantime. Jeff Beck, in particular, produces an as of now ultimate, heartbreaking cover for his Memphis-based *Jeff Beck Group* (1972). It is probably mainly thanks to the producer, Booker T. & the M.G.'s guitarist Steve Cropper, that this is one of the most successful exercises in the sound that Beck so desperately seeks in these years, the definitive blend of Memphis soul, Chicago blues and British rock.

Tina Turner operates in the same A-category, and with her debut solo album *Tina Turns The Country On!* (1974) she tries to tap into a new audience - the Nashville audience, to be precise. With covers of Kristofferson ("Help Me Make It Through the Night"), Hank Snow and Dolly Parton... and two Dylan songs: "*He Belongs To Me*" and "Tonight I'll Be Staying Here With You". It doesn't really match up, Tina's excited, scintillating vocals on the one hand and the friendly steel guitar parts, the neat bass lines and conveyor belt drumming on the other, but it does get attention; it earns her a Grammy nomination.

To no avail. Dylan is adamant and cannot be tempted into putting the song on his set list in January 1974. Indeed, at none of the 40 concerts of that American tour with The Band the song is performed - apparently the promotion of "Tonight I'll Be Staying Here With You" to *Greatest Hit* was just a whim after all. A fling. A one-night stand.

But soon it'll be 1975, and thunder will be rolling...

VI   A mattress and sand letters

Throw my ticket out the window
Throw my suitcase out there, too
Throw my troubles out the door
I don't need them anymore
'cause tonight I'll be staying here with you

Throw my ticket in the wind
Throw my mattress out there too
Draw my letters in the sand,
'cause you got to understand
that tonight I'll be staying here with you

The Rolling Thunder Revue kicks off in late October 1975, and one of the many pleasant surprises is the live debut of "Tonight I'll Be Staying Here With You" at the 22nd concert of the tour, on Saturday, November 22 in Waltham, Massachusetts. Surprising, this rehabilitation, but even more remarkable is the complete, sweeping restoration; almost every verse has been changed. And there is a third surprise, which seems to be a present for the steadily growing army of Dylanologists.

The first two more serious Dylan biographies were published in the previous years (Toby Thompson's *Positively Main Street: An unorthodox view of Bob Dylan* and Anthony Scaduto's *Bob Dylan*, both 1972). And Dylan, of course, has had plenty to contend with, from the likes of A.J. Weberman, the garbage scavenger, to the intrusive fans who think they can invade his privacy, to the remorseless, bootlicking "journalists", who all think they can distil the most intimate private matters from his song lyrics. Heroin addiction, homosexuality, anarchistic beliefs, messianic qualities, adultery... you name it. Dylan's image and the misty quality of many of his lyrics unleash a great deal of creativity and obsessiveness, and correspondingly many painfully stupid conclusions about the man's private life - mostly because a significant faction of Dylanologists stubbornly believes that every "I" in the songs is "*I, Bob Dylan*".

As if to trigger that faction, Dylan announces the song twice with a teaser. "The next one is also a true story," he says 27 November in Bangor, after "The Lonesome Death Of Hattie Carroll". And four days later, in Toronto: "Here's another true story comin' up."

It gives extra weight to the second surprise, to the textual changes. At least, it does suggest that Dylan has deleted the "untrue" elements, and that the text has become "true" because of these corrections. In any case, it is immediately clear that Dylan took the revision seriously. In the first verse, for instance, the metre is corrected - it is still trochaic tetrameters, but each line now has a correctly stressed, masculine, ending. In the original lyrics, the opening line still had an unstressed, feminine ending. It seems to explain the rather meaningless change from "out the window" to "in the wind".

Less traceable is the utterly radical change of verse two, from "Throw my suitcase out there, too" to "Throw my mattress out there too". Technically almost identical; same number of syllables, same rhythm, male ending, but for some reason a scratching and rewriting Dylan has changed *suitcase* to *mattress*. Stylistically, a minor, insignificant enhancement with a thin alliteration (*my mattress*), but that debatable enhancement is completely overshadowed by the quite drastic change to the enigmatic command of the I-person, who demands that his apparently strong and muscular mistress throws out his mattress - for otherwise unclear reasons. But, mind you, this is "a true story". So maybe it was an air mattress. Still, apart from the presumed physical challenge the antagonist is facing here, the symbolism is particularly disturbing: the removal of the lover's sleeping place does not at all match the love message *tonight I'll be staying here with you.*

It is a fairly recent intervention. On CD1 of *The Bootleg Series 15 - The Rolling Thunder Revue* (2019), we can listen to the rehearsal of the song on 19 October in New York, and here there is no mention of a *mattress*. The line there is "Throw my troubles out there too", and no mattress appears in the rest of the lyrics either. The same applies to the equally curious follow-up line, *Draw my letters in the sand*. This line is not sung in the rehearsal either, and ambiguous it is as well, to say the least. After all, *letters in the sand* signal transience, brevity, impermanence. In fact, since 1957, since Pat Boone scored a major hit with the time-honoured "Love Letters In The Sand", an inescapable connotation - and Dylan, who most likely has Gene Austin's 1931 version on a pedestal, knows that too.

It is, all in all, a somewhat alienating rewriting. In the rest of the lyrics almost every line has been rewritten too, but those rewritings are all in line with the protagonist's original state of love. "Your love was all that mattered", for instance, and "You came down on me like rolling thunder". There is no "leakage" from other songs either, as is sometimes the case with Dylan. The surrounding songs in this show, and during the tour in general, are all mattress-less and sandletter-free. At most, "mattress" recalls 1966's "Leopard-Skin Pill-Box Hat", recalls the bizarre line "You know it balances on your head just like a mattress balances on a bottle of wine" - apparently, the mere word "mattress" inspires frenzies. And Dylan used it before as an attribute to represent exceptional physical strength of the female counterpart:

> "love is gentleness – softness - creaminess" says Phaedra - who is now having a pillow fight - her weapon, a mattress - she stands on a deserted marshmallow,"

...like in his poetic prose explosion *Tarantula*, in which Phaedra does not, as it should be, swings a pillow during a pillow fight, but the whole mattress.

On the other hand, perhaps Dylan's mind is again "normally" haunted by Johnny Cash, who recently had a minor hit with the potentially charming, but unfortunately rather overproduced (saccharine violins, terrible ladies' choir) "Papa Was a Good Man";

> *It rained all the way to Cincinnati*
> *With our mattress on top of the car*
> *Us kids were eatin' crackers and baloney*
> *And papa kept on driving never stopped once at a ba*r

Little in common with "Tonight I'll Be Staying Here With You", that's true. But that mattress has to come from *somewhere*.

VII A Spider's Life On Mars

I should have left this town this morning
But it was more than I could do
Oh, your love comes on so strong
And I've waited all day long
For tonight when I'll be staying here with you

I could have left this town by noon
By tonight I'd been to someplace new
But I was feeling a little bit scattered
And your love was all that mattered
So tonight I'll be staying here with you

More drastic than any textual change, of course, is the musical turnaround. On *Nashville Skyline*, "Tonight I'll Be Staying Here With You" is a melodic mid-tempo country ballad, Dylan using his new crooner voice and singing with the brakes on. Colour is added by long steel guitar strokes, the piano suggests some debauchery and the only - modest - fireworks come from the electric guitar (Norman Blake, by the sound of it).

But at the *Rolling Thunder Revue*, six years later, we have Mick Ronson on stage.

Mick Ronson is probably the most famous Hullensian, although a remarkable number of notable people come from the relatively small city of Hull, or rather: Kingston upon Hull (about 260,000 inhabitants). Who then also usually show a kind of regional pride. Songwriter Phillip Goodhand-Tait writes "Lincoln County", the popular 80s band The Housemartins give their successful debut album the witty title *London 0 Hull 4* and Ronson calls his third, posthumously released album *Heaven And Hull* (1994). On which, by the way, one of the few tolerable covers of "Like A Rolling Stone" can be found, sung by David Bowie.

A cynic might think that *Heaven And Hull* is not too complimentary, but Ronson means well. And so it is understood; after his death (29 April 1993, liver cancer), the city honours him with a Memorial Stage in Queen's Gardens, a guitar sculpture in East Park and a wonderful memorial rock show, *Turn And Face The Strange*, performed 22 times in 2017, 2018 and 2019 to sold-out audiences each time.

It is fitting that Ronson's musical life should end with Bowie - after all, the Spider From Mars also emerged in the shadow of Ziggy Stardust in the early 1970s.

Before *Ziggy Stardust*, on Bowie's *Hunky Dory*, Ronson really shines for the first time. As a child, he learned to play the recorder, piano, harmonium and violin, and that diverse upbringing now pays off. And his talent, of course - a brilliant string arrangement like in "Life On Mars?" requires more than just skill. The exceptional beauty of "Life On Mars?" is in any case largely due to *Ronno*. The rough demo recording, with only Bowie on piano, already reveals that it's a beautiful song, but it only becomes a *hors category* song because of Ronson's recorder (second verse), both guitar solos and above all the strings - remarkably his very first string arrangement, which he nervously had written out note for note with sweaty hands for the arrogant studio musicians of the BBC. Especially admirable given the complex chord progression and the widely varying melody lines - it's not a ten-a-penny song that Ronson arranges so masterfully, so sumptuously.

Van Morrison, Mott The Hoople, Elton John, Morrissey... Ronson's name as a go-to guy is established. Even more so after he turns out to be able to surpass the high school art of his masterpiece *Hunky Dory* on *Ziggy Stardust* (on "Five Years", piano, autoharp, electric guitar, backing vocals and string arrangement are all his, for instance), and then on Lou Reed's bestseller *Transformer* (1973) - yep, that's Ronno's piano, recorder and string arrangements again, on again outer category pop songs, on "Perfect Day" and "Satellite Of Love".

Wonderful, moving arrangements by a classically trained prodigy - but at heart Ronson has always remained a rock 'n' roller. We hear that in both the nippy lead guitar parts of Reed's "Vicious", in the straightforward sweaty rock of Bowie's "Hang On To Yourself" and "Suffragette City", in the neurotic solo on Elton John's "Madman Across The Water" - and with Dylan, on the stage of the *Rolling Thunder Revue*.

On a social, personal level, there seems to be no special connection with Dylan, although according to Sam Shepard's wonderful *Rolling Thunder Logbook*, Ronson is the "chief instigator of the make-up craze which swept through Rolling Thunder like a brush fire". But musically, there is all the more of a click - and the reanimated "Tonight I'll Be Staying Here With You" is one of the best examples thereof.

"Ronson," Shepard notes in the same *Logbook* about the *Night Of The Hurricane* concert,

> "really gets off on this monster crowd. Slashing his guitar with huge full-arm uppercuts. Platinum-blond hair spraying in all directions. Then stalking across the stage, stiff legged, Frankenstein macho strutting, shaking the neck of his guitar with his vicious chord hand as though throttling his weaker brother. All the time, never losing a lick. Through every motion playing genius, inspirational lead lines."

... *genius, inspirational lead lines* of his characteristic Gibson Les Paul with that characteristic full-bodied, slightly floating sound. And that inspiring fire also seems to ignite Dylan's vocals; the difference between Dylan the elderly crooner from Nashville and Dylan the syllable-spitting, splattering rocker from the *Rolling Thunder Revue* is immense. Debatable, sure, but a significant faction of fans considers Dylan's singing on this tour a highlight in his long concert history - and there is something to be said for that. Dylan sings "Tonight I'll Be Staying Here With You" with the passion of a smitten, fierce rock god - and that seems to help influence the otherwise insignificant changes in content. Like in this second verse; *"I could"* sounds more energetic, louder, than the original *"I should"*, like *"leaving by noon"* fits a creature of the night more than *"leaving by morning"*, like *"scattered"* is a great word to hurl enthusiastically through a wall of guitar violence into the concert hall. Better than *"Oh, your love comes on so strong"*, anyway.

After the Rolling Thunder tour, Ronson gives his guitar to one of his biggest fans, Mick Rossi from punk rock band Slaughter And The Dogs. An anonymous collector from Manchester gets his hands on it, but thankfully lends it to the temporary exhibition and performance *Turn And Face The Strange* in Hull.

"Mick's Rolling Thunder Les Paul," says the exhibition sign. She is a shining centrepiece.

VIII   On The 309

Is it really any wonder
The love that a stranger might receive
You cast your spell and I went under
I find it so difficult to leave

Is it really any wonder
the changes we put on each other's heads
You came down on me like rolling thunder
I left my dreams on the riverbed

The second alienating, radical textual change, after that mattress-slinging village beauty from the opening couplet, is the closing line of the bridge. Of course, almost every line in the 1975 Rolling Thunder version has been radically changed, in the sense that they are all different words, but the tenor is almost the same as the original. *Throw my ticket in the wind* is not much different from *Throw my ticket out*

the window, and *I could have left this town by noon* communicates in other words the same as *I should have left this town by morning*, to name but two examples.

That also applies to the bridge, at first. *Stranger* and *changes* are related, *You cast your spell and I went under* has the same emotional charge as *You came down on me like rolling thunder* - with the wordplay reference to the name of the tour as a bonus (which is appreciated by the audience with somewhat exaggerated hilarity).

I left my dreams on the riverbed, however, suddenly takes a turn that is radically different from the message *I find it so difficult to leave*. The latter is a tender, loving expression of an infatuation; the revision, taken in isolation, expresses a rather bitter resignation – "*leaving your dreams*" is far from romantic in any case. *Riverbed*, while somewhat strange, can be understood as an insider's wink at "a bed in a house by the river" or something like that. Anyhow, *riverbed* does not have an unambiguous, commonly understood connotation. A vague Western association at most. Dylan himself has used the word once before, not so long ago by the way, in "Lily, Rosemary And The Jack Of Hearts";

> *Two doors down the boys finally made it through the wall*
> *And cleaned out the bank safe, it's said that they got off with*
> *quite a haul*
> *In the darkness by the riverbed they waited on the ground*
> *For one more member who had business back in town*
> *But they couldn't go no further without the Jack of Hearts*

So Dylan himself seems to have that vague Western association as well: a riverbed is a piece of scenery for a nineteenth-century scene somewhere in the Wild West. Just like Johnny Cash (in "All Around Cowboy"; *he's dry as an old riverbed*) or the Irish cowboy Van Morrison in "Moonshine Whiskey" (*I just want to lay my feet on a river bed*). Or Doug Kershaw's hit "Louisiana Man" - which somewhere in Dylan's inner jukebox is sung by Johnny Cash, Buck Owens, Ricky Nelson, Jan & Dean, and an array of others. The most beautiful perhaps by the irresistible Bobbie Gentry;

> *At birth mom and papa called their little boy Ned*
> *Raised him on the banks of a river bed*
> *On a houseboat tied to a big tall tree*
> *A home for my papa and my mama and me*

... wherein, however, the emotional charge of *riverbed* drifts far from the tenor of Dylan's song. *I left my dreams behind* has a melancholic, maybe even a bit bitter, overtone. But then again: maybe Dylan just shouts something out of the blue, filler lyrics - at the rehearsal in New York, a month earlier, this line did not yet exist. Dylan sings something partly unintelligible there (*I finally .... so true*, something like that), but nothing about lost dreams and riverbeds, in any case.

The remainder of the revised text, the third stanza, gives no reason either to think that the strange closing line of the bridge was a well-thought-out textual intervention:

> *I can hear that lonesome whistle blowin'*
> *I hear them semis rolling too*
> *If there's a driver on the road*
> *Better let him have my load*
> *cause tonight I'll be staying here with you*

...the meaning of which is pretty much the same a month earlier, in the rehearsal:

> *I can hear that lonesome whistle blowin'*
> *I can hear those semi-trucks rollin' too*
> *If there's a cowboy on the plane*
> *then let him have my train*
> *cause tonight I'll be staying here with you*

An anecdotal change from *train* to the Rolling Thunder Revue's mode of transport, with the resulting disappearance of the *stationmaster* and the *poor boy* in favour of a *driver* or a *cowboy*... it's not too earth-shattering. No hint of a clue, anyway, as to why or which dreams were abandoned in the preceding bridge. Still, Dylan seems to be quite content with that anecdotal shift from *train* to *semi-trucks*. The original from '69 closes with a repeat of the first verse, of the *throw my ticket out the window* verse. During the first performance of the song at the Rolling Thunder Revue, he decides to repeat this last *semi-truck* verse.

Maybe because he thinks it's the first rock song to use the word *semi-truck*, who knows. Though in fact he is just beaten on that front by Tom Waits and his cover of Red Sovine's 1967 hit, "Big Joe and Phantom 309" (*Nighthawks At The Diner*, 1975). Waits is fairly faithful to the lyrics of the original, touching ghost story about the friendly spirit of Big Joe who picks up hitchhikers in his truck Phantom 309, entertaining them with his stories, but Waits changes one small detail:

> *He pushed her ahead with 10 forward gears*
> *Man that dashboard was lit like the old*
> *Madam La Rue pinball, a serious semi truck*

... he turns Red Sovine's *truck* into a *semi-truck*.

In 2003, Johnny Cash writes his last song, the masterful "Like The 309", which is released only three years after his death (on *American V: A Hundred Highways*, 2006). Cash borrows "309", obviously, from "Big Joe and Phantom 309", but turns the truck back into a train. Johnny wrote his very first song in 1954 about a train journey ("Hey Porter"), and Johnny writes his very last song about a train journey again, fifty years later - about his coffin that will be taken on the *309* to its final resting place. Probably because Johnny Cash, just like Dylan, needs to hear the steam whistle blow:

> *I hear the sound of a railroad train*
> *The whistle blows and I'm gone again*
> *Hitman, take me higher than a Georgia pine*
> *Stand back children, it's the 309*
> *It's the 309, it's the 309*
> *Put me in my box on the 309*

Yep, *I can hear that steam whistle blowin'*.

IX   Music from the Big Mushroom

evil charlatans masquerading in pullover vests & tuxedos talking gobbledyook

(Bob Dylan, *World Gone Wrong*, 1993)

The spirit of Bob Dylan hovers throughout the British Charlatans' oeuvre anyway, and openly and unashamedly comes to the fore on their successful fifth album, *Tellin' Stories* (1997). The album is stuffed with references to Dylan songs, like in the answer song to "Like A Rolling Stone", the more melancholy "Get On It" (*no matter how you're feeling, you're never on your own*), like in The Charlatans' cheerful answer to "Girl Of The North Country", the swaggering "North Country Boy" (*I threw it all away / I don't know where I put it / But I miss it all the same*) and as in the charming, understated Dylan reverence "You're A Big Girl Now", probably the only other song in the world with the word combination "jet pilot eyes";

See her through jet pilot eyes
Mysterious and thin
Like a raven breakin' free
From the towers they keep you in

... borrowed from the obscure 1965 outtake "Jet Pilot Eyes", which The Charlatans know from *Biograph*. That compilation box leaves more traces, by the way. For the intro of "Blue For You" (*Up At The Lake*, 2004), guitarist Mark Collins boldly incorporates *Biograph*'s live version of "Isis", for instance.

And the box set inspires the October 2021 release of their own *Biograph*-like box set, *A Head Full of Ideas: The Best of Charlatans*; "We were all at The Charlatans studio and there was a Bob Dylan box set lying around and it was there shouting at me that we should do one of these," singer Tim Burgess tells *Headliner*. That studio of The Charlatans is called Big Mushroom - a nod to the Big Pink. The name of the box set, *A Head Full Of Ideas*, is a line from their biggest hit "One To Another" (1997), the song whose last verse opens with the familiar words *Can you please crawl out your window*.

In his 2012 autobiographical book, also titled *Tellin' Stories*, Tim Burgess then reveals that *Biograph* actually marks a kind of beginning for The Charlatans:

> "Martin Kelly and I became inseparable at this time. I remember going to his flat in Ladbroke Grove and spending the whole evening talking about Bob Dylan. I was into Dylan, and getting in deeper. Martin pulled out Biograph and asked me whether I had it. I didn't. He played me 'You're a Big Girl Now', a version only available as part of this box set. Martin thought it was the best thing Dylan had ever done. He had two copies of Biograph, a CD and vinyl, and he generously gave me the vinyl. Mates for life!"

(Chapter 4: Garlic Bread and Britpop)

Tellin' Stories is followed by the somewhat snowed under *Us And Us Only* (1999), an album with at least as much staying power as its predecessor, and with even more and even stronger traces of Dylan - not only in the lyrics, but now also in the music. Still pleasantly unobtrusive, and still loving.

The Dylan worship starts already in the opening song, in the hypnotic "Forever". The long, instrumental intro mainly evokes associations with The Stones' *Their Satanic Majesties Request*, but when Tim Burgess starts singing after 2'38", he soon returns to his Bob roots: *Love is all there is* (from "I Threw It All Away"), *I wonder what you people do with your lives* (paraphrasing "Tangled Up In Blue"), *I see my true love coming, my little bundle of joy* (quoting "Down Along The Cove")... and like this, there are more half and whole references to Dylan's catalogue. The opening song is followed by a trio of songs that form the most Dylanesque trio in The Charlatans' output. "Sounds like Bob Dylan and The Band on ecstasy playing at the last night of the Heavenly Social," as bassist Martin Blunt admits in an interview with *New Musical Express* (15 June 1999).

"Impossible" is one of the best mercurial-period-Dylan songs not written by Dylan. Every verse seems to come from an unreleased *Blonde On Blonde* song. From the opening verse onwards;

> *Impossible raw women*
> *I you know you're all too hard to please*
> *I can help you*
> *If you only ask me kindly*
> *Don't make me get down on my knees*
> *God bless these hungry women*
> *Impossible to ever keep*
> *Your breath has never tasted as sweet*

... up to shining Dylanesque put-downs like *Y'know he looks like a plastic surgeon* and *Your new friend he seems to love you / I hope he cries himself to sleep*. All framed by acoustic guitar, Al Kooper-like organ playing and Nashville piano. Plus, for dessert, a perfect imitation of Dylan's harmonica playing.

The song flows smoothly, in many ways, into the next track, "The Blonde Waltz". Again acoustic guitar, mercurial organ and piano, the title is lovingly stolen from *Tarantula* (chapter 40, "Subterranean Homesick Blues & the Blonde Waltz") and the opening line is the biggest giveaway: *Oh! my love my darling young son*... "A Hard Rain's A-Gonna Fall" revisited. After which one subtle hint after another follows (*I heard the sound of thunder in the place where all the poets sing*, for instance).

And the "Dylan terzet" closes with the beautiful rock song "A House Is Not A Home". With the most catchy tribute to Dylan: the driving lick is love & theft from "I Don't Believe You". The song is again embellished with the by now usual half-quotes and paraphrases (*I can't believe this is the end* and *blowing on your trumpet* from Blonde On Blonde, and *I think I used a little too much force* from "Tangled Up In Blue", for example), but that half *I Don't Believe You*-lick is the real anchor.

The Dylan storm then seems to die down a bit. In tracks 6, 7 and 8 ("Senses", "My Beautiful Friend" and "I Don't Care Where You Live"), one or two modest Dylan references pass by (*Our lives are a-changin'*, for example), but towards the end of the album, on track 9, the hurricane picks up again. The wonderful "The Blind Stagger" is actually much more than a vehicle for a few sympathetic Dylan references: the song is in fact one big tribute to the great hero of The Charlatans. Take a fragment like

*You're invisible, is there something I can give to you
I see my light come shining
There is good on the horizon*

*Daylight sneaking through my window
I will give you a rainbow and a bucket full of gold
You've been bitten by eleven hungry kittens
Who will go the whole distance while the blind stagger*

... which is successively cut and pasted from fragments of "Like A Rolling Stone", "Boots Of Spanish Leather", "I Shall Be Released", "You're A Big Girl Now", "Watching The River Flow" and "A Hard Rain's A-Gonna Fall". More subtle is the reverence in the musical setting; the chord progression *G-G7-C-G6*, on which the song rests, seems to be inspired by Dylan's most favourite chord scheme – the bard does use the *G-G6-G7* figure in combination with the *C* in dozens of songs. "Percy's Song", "With God On Our Side", "My Back Pages", "Don't Think Twice", "The Times", "Hattie Carroll", "Restless Farewell", "To Ramona", "I Don't Believe You", "Mama You Been On My Mind"... you probably can't find a chord combination that Dylan uses more often than this one.

The lyrics to the opening couplet of "The Blind Stagger" are no less Dylanesque;

*Lord, it's been a long, long time
And people don't you find always leave their troubles at your door
I, I live on my own
I don't need a bitter soul beatin' on about my country anymore
Don't you think your daddy needs you home right away
Your daddy needs you home right away*

... the most striking is of course the last line, copied from the early masterpiece "I Was Young When I Left Home". But almost unnoticed, the "Tonight I'll Be Staying Here With You" reference to *throw my troubles out the door* slips through. It leads to the only

Dylan cover The Charlatans recorded in the studio (2002), to one of the most beautiful "Tonight I'll Be Staying Here With You" covers of the twenty-first century. Borne by the extraordinarily beautiful, driving Hammond organ, larded with elusive *Madchester* psychedelia, especially in the bridge, and above all: Burgess' irresistible, weirdly attractive singing, alternating back-and-forth between falsetto and tenor.

The Japanese release of *Us And Us Alone*, by the way, has two more great bonus tracks. "Your Precious Love", The Charlatans' version of "Tombstone Blues", and "Sleepy Little Sunshine Boy", in which Burgess wishes the sunshine boy: *may you grow up to be righteous*. Yes, Dylan staying forever young is also thanks to the love of The Charlatans.

X   Smooching with Lisa Bonet

Nick Hornby is a justly celebrated writer and talented scriptwriter whose own books are often made into very enjoyable films by other scriptwriters. *About A Boy, Fever Pitch, A Long Way Down*... but the real success began with the film adaptation of his first novel, *High Fidelity* (book 1995, film 2000, musical 2006, television series 2020). Autobiographical elements shine through enough, but most clearly in protagonist Rob's obsessive tendency to make Top 5 lists of everything. The book even opens therewith;

> "My desert-island, all-time, top five most memorable split-ups, in chronological order:
> > *1) Alison Ashworth*
> > *2) Penny Hardwick*
> > *3) Jackie Allen*
> > *4) Charlie Nicholson*
> > *5) Sarah Kendrew*
>
> These were the ones that really hurt."

How fond Nick Hornby himself is of making lists, he shows in 2003, with the publication of *31 Songs*, a beautiful collection of essays on his 31 favourite songs. In it, he also expresses his awkward, very two-faced relationship with Dylan's records. In the opening line to Favourite Song No. 8, Dylan's "Can You Please Crawl Out Your Window?", he is quite clear: "I'm not a big Dylan fan." A stroll through his record collection, however, reveals, to his own surprise, that he has some twenty CDs by Dylan – "in fact I own more recordings by Dylan than by any other artist." And when discussing Favourite Song No. 7, Rod Stewart's cover of the Dylan song "Mama You Been On My Mind", the *not-a-big-Dylan fan* drops:

> "Dylan's 'Mama You Been On My Mind' seems to me to be not much more than a strum - an exquisite strum, with one of Dylan's loveliest and simplest lyrics, but a strum nonetheless. Stewart's evident love for the song rescues it, or at least spotlights it: where Dylan almost throws it away, with the implication that there's plenty more where that one came from, Stewart's reverence seems to dignify it, invest it with an epical quality Dylan denies it."

That same special talent, the talent to express admiration with highly quotable, cast-iron sentences, Hornby demonstrates again in Chapter 8, the chapter on "Can You Please Crawl Out Your Window?": *There's a density and a gravity to a Dylan song that you can't find anywhere else.*

In the book *High Fidelity*, however, Dylan is not mentioned too often. About four times. Very respectful, though: "All-time top five favourite recording artists: Madness, Eurythmics, Bob Dylan, Joni Mitchell, Bob Marley." And Dylan is explicitly linked to Rob's emotional struggles once:

> "When I get home (twenty quid, Putney to Crouch End, and no tip) I make myself a cup of tea, plug in the headphones, and plow through every angry song about women by Bob Dylan and Elvis Costello I own."

Striking enough, in any case, for the screenwriters to highlight Dylan more in the otherwise very faithful film adaptation. "Most Of The Time", under the romantic climax, in the pouring rain after a funeral vigil late at night, makes the most impression. The song from 1989 was covered once until the filming, by Lloyd Cole in 1995. After the success of the film and the soundtrack, it has been covered more than twenty times (most beautifully by Sophie Zelmani in 2003, but the raw, unadorned cover by ex-Grandaddy Jason Lytle in 2021 also has its own distinctive emotional power).

In the scenario Dylan's name pops up as well, every now and then. Like in the witty shop scene in which Barry (Jack Black) pushes one must-have album after another into the hands of a dorky customer:

> "You don't have it? That is perverse. Don't tell anybody you don't own fucking Blonde On Blonde [*stacking the album on the pile in the hands of the overwhelmed customer*]. It's gonna be okay."

And on the soundtrack, one more Dylan song comes along: "Tonight I'll Be Staying Here With You", under the sensual love scene Rob has with a one-night stand, the enchanting singer/

songwriter Marie DeSalle. Played, incidentally, by the secret childhood crush of half the Western world's population over 40, Lisa "Denise Huxtable" Bonet. To complete the circle, the lead role in *High Fidelity*'s 2020 television adaptation is played by Zoë Kravitz, Lisa Bonet's equally enchanting daughter from her marriage to Lenny Kravitz.

The splashing *Rolling Thunder* performance of the song did not really lead to a broad, general reappraisal of the song at the time. From the 70s, only the 1979 version by British blues veteran Dave Kelly is worth mentioning. An unadventurous, country-like arrangement, true, but it's all the first years after the *Rolling Thunder Revue* have to offer. And it *does* have a pleasantly nostalgic piano.

In the 80s, the song remains just as obscure. Dylan himself never plays it, his colleagues also ignore "Tonight I'll Be Staying Here With You". With one exception: the energetic soul veteran Nappy Brown experiences a come-back in the 80s, some thirty years after his glory years (between 1954 and '58 he scored his biggest hits). After Jeff Beck, Cher and Esther Williams, Nappy is the next to recognize the soul potential of the song and records a catchy, swinging mid-tempo soul stomp for his strong album *Tore Up* (1984).

From 1990 onwards, Dylan plays it himself again, at irregular intervals, and that, plus perhaps the reasonably successful cover of Albert Lee (1991), leads to a steady reappraisal.

In the course of the 90s, the song then appears here and there on the setlist of Second Division artists, until Premier League player and Dylan disciple Jimmy LaFave reanimates it completely in

1999, in turn inciting the blues potential, but above all - as usual - appealing because of his husky, skipping vocals and his unique phrasing.

The film adaptation of *High Fidelity* then seems, as it did for "Most Of The Time", to throw open the gate once and for all; after 2000, "Tonight I'll Be Staying Here With You" enters the canon. In all categories, too; blues, country and rock artists, of course. A forgotten recording by Rick Nelson from 1969 surfaces, as a bonus track on the reissue of *Rick Nelson In Concert* (2011). In jazz circles as well, as in a somewhat safe, sultry, but not unattractive rendition by Janet Planet. And soul, especially soul - which usually makes for very attractive covers, as the delightful Ann Peebles proves, with old master Allen Toussaint on the piano in 2005. En passant demonstrating why the old soul diva ("I Can't Stand The Rain") is inducted into the Memphis Music Hall of Fame in 2014.

However, its particular beauty is best appreciated in a hybrid, in a mash-up of rock, soul, blues and country, as Jeff Beck argued half a century ago. For an exercise in that winning category we have to go to continental Europe, to a small town in the south of Holland. In Breda, Jan Barten and Fons Havermans produce Dylan covers, in which the Muscle Shoals-like piano, funky guitar, driving Hammond organ, Kenny Buttrey drums and jazz-rock-ish Steely Dan guitar solos create the perfect blend of Memphis, Nashville and New York. Their "One Of Us Must Know" with brilliant, percussive Stevie Wonder keyboard work is a great example of that approach, and "Tonight I'll Be Staying Here With You" emulates the warmth and drive.

Tonight I'll Be Staying Here With You" never made it to the *real* top, though. In a - fictitious - list of Most Covered Dylan Songs, the song probably only just makes it to the Top 30 - at best, it 's a mid-tier. And apparently, only Dylan's original has the magical power to give even a sucker like Rob Gordon the chance to make out with Lisa Bonet... after which he'll be staying with her tonight, the lucky devil.

Tuesday, February 18, 1969
Columbia Recording Studios
Nashville, Tennessee

Produced by Bob Johnston

Take 1 – 2
One Too Many Mornings

Take 3 – 4
Mountain Dew (Bascom Lamar Lunsford/Scott Wiseman)

Take 5 – 8
I Still Miss Someone (Johnny Cash/Roy Cash Jr.)

Take 9
Careless Love (Trad.)

Take 10 – 12
Matchbox

Take 13 – 14
That's All Right Mama (Arthur Crudup)

Take 15
Mystery Train

Take 16 – 17
Big River (Johnny Cash)

Take 18 – 20
Girl From The North Country

Take 21 – 22
I Walk The Line (Johnny Cash)

Take 23
How High The Water (Johnny Cash)

Take 24
You Are My Sunshine (Jimmy Davis/Charles Mitchell)

Take 25 – 27
Ring Of Fire (June Carter/Merle Kilgore)

Take 28
Wanted Man

Take 29 – 33
Guess Things Happen That Way (Jack Clement)

Take 34 – 35
Amen

Take 36
Just A Closer Walk With Thee (Trad.)

Take 37 – 38
Blue Yodel # 1 (Jimmie Rodgers)

Musicians:
Johnny Cash (vocals and guitar), Carl Perkins (guitar), Bob Wootton (guitar), Marshall Grant (bass), W.S. Holland (drums)

11 Girl From The North Country

I   He was a real magpie

The sympathetic English folk giant Martin Carthy has an admirable talent for getting to the point with perfect metaphors. As to characterise an exceptional quality of young Dylan:

> "He was a real magpie, but he had this wonderful creativity that went along with it. [...] What he had was a memory like a piece of blotting paper. If somebody sang something that he thought was wonderful, he'd go back to his hotel and write down what he remembered. It might come out as a new song, but that's where it would be from."
> (*Tradfolk* interview, 28 February 2018)

"He was a real magpie" is a wonderful, comprehensive image. Typifying not only the young trouba-dour with whom Carthy roams London from one folk club to another, but actually the old one as well. The magpie who picks up the shiny bits and takes them to his nest to build his own work of art. And Carthy illustrates his memories with familiar and less familiar examples. I heard him, he tells us, singing *"Where have you been my blue-eyed son?"*, and thought he was playing "Lord Randall" - until three seconds later I realised it was "A Hard Rain's A-Gonna Fall".

Dylan's incredible memory for songs, as well as his lovingly copy/paste talent, has of course been spotted often enough as well, but rarely as evocatively as by Carthy: "What he had was a memory like a piece of blotting paper." And reconstructing those memories, those quickly stored impressions, back in his hotel room, then become the basis for what "might come out as a new song". In which he exposes a creative process, as it is described by the 62-year-old Dylan himself too, in the Robert Hilburn interview for the *LA Times*, November 2003 in Amsterdam:

> "I'll be playing Bob Nolan's 'Tumbling Tumbleweeds,' for instance, in my head constantly — while I'm driving a car or talking to a person or sitting around or whatever. People will think they are talking to me and I'm talking back, but I'm not. I'm listening to the song in my head. At a certain point, some of the words will change and I'll start writing a song."

Incidentally, it is hard to find a song in Dylan's oeuvre that features a "changed" "Tumbling Tumbleweeds". "Rollin' And Tumblin'" seems obvious, but doesn't fit - in terms of atmosphere and pace, songs like "Life Is Hard" or "Moonlight" come closer, but presumably Dylan just mentions a song that comes to mind at this moment, during this interview.

However, there are plenty of songs in Dylan's oeuvre where it is abundantly clear what the template is, of course. The old Irish drinking song "The Parting Glass" for "Restless Farewell", for example, "Nottamun Town" becomes "Masters Of War", or "No More Auction Block" for "Blowin' In The Wind"; there are dozens of examples. And one of the most famous and celebrated is "Scarborough Fair", from which Dylan sculpted one of his all-time greatest, "Girl From The Country". According to lore, anyway.

"Scarborough Fair" was "my thing", says Carthy. Every artist in that folk circle in the late 50s had his own "signature song", so to speak. Davey Graham had "Angi" (or "Anji" or "Angie"), Bert Jansch "Strolling Down The Highway" and Carthy had "Scarborough Fair". He stopped playing it himself ("too much baggage"), but:

> "I love the fact that Bob Dylan got 'Girl From the North Country'
> from it. It was very typical of him to do that – very him. In fact,
> he came back and he said [*cue Bob Dylan impersonation*], "I
> wanna sing you this!" And he started to sing it, and he was
> trying to do the guitar figure. He got halfway through the first
> verse and he said, "Oh man, I can't do this!" [*Laughs*] He wasn't
> really ready. He was just so excited about it."

... and that "Scarborough Fair" was more or less taken away from him by Paul Simon doesn't really bother him anymore either: "It was my signature piece, but it's a traditional song, for god's sake! Why shouldn't he do it?" When Paul Simon performs in London in 1998, he apparently remembers a debt of honour, and invites Martin on stage to play the song together. The generous Carthy is happy to oblige.

Like Simon, Dylan is still aware of Carthy's contribution decades after the fact, as evidenced by his words in the *Rolling Stone* interview in 1984:

> "But I ran into some people in England who really knew those
> songs. Martin Carthy, another guy named Nigel Davenport.
> Martin Carthy's incredible. I learned a lot of stuff from Martin.
> Girl From The North Country is based on a song I heard him sing
> - that Scarborough Fair song, which Paul Simon, I guess, just
> took the whole thing."

Which, by the way, contradicts his own quote in Nat Hentoff's liner notes on *The Freewheelin'*. Hentoff writes there:

> "Girl From The North Country was first conceived by Bob Dylan
> about three years before he finally wrote it down in December
> 1962."

... and then quotes Dylan, who implicitly confirms this genesis: "That often happens. I carry a song in my head for a long time and then it comes bursting out." Which is then rebutted by both Carthy and Dylan himself, and a first superficial song comparison indeed does demonstrate it; Dylan must have turned the old folk song into "Girl From The North Country" in the same days that he was introduced to Carthy's version of "Scarborough Fair", December '62. That he would have walked around with it for "about three years" is one of the many fables peddled in those liner notes. And actually, the gravity of the template is a bit overblown as well.

The plot of "Scarborough Fair", the dialogue about a love that can only be won if the other accomplishes impossible tasks (sewing *a seamless cambric shirt*, finding *an acre of land* between the salty seawater and the wet beach) evaporates, to be saved, in a way, for the equally stunningly beautiful sister of the girl from the North, for "Boots Of Spanish Leather". A few phrases are taken verbatim - but not many; only *Remember me to one who lives there / For once she was a true love of mine*, in fact. And the melody may be an echo, though not much more than that - the outline is recognisable, but the harmonic structure is really different. And so is the time signature - Scarborough is played in 6/8 or 3/4, Dylan plays an ordinary 4/4 metre. There are, in any case, plenty of songs in Dylan's discography that are much more faithful to the template than "Girl From The North Country" is to "Scarborough Fair". It is, in short, defensible that Dylan considers the song an own creation. Which, incidentally, Carthy implicitly acknowledges when he says:

> "He did actually annoy some people by being such an effective piece of blotting paper. I don't understand that, personally. I think it's fantastic. Somebody suggested that "Blowin' In The Wind" was actually a reworking of a tune called "No More Auction Block". I've no idea if that's true. There's only a limited number of notes in the scale, aren't there? You gonna trip over each other at some point."
>
> (interview for *Prism Films*, 2013)

II   La Gazza Ladra

Ornithomancy it is called, divination based on bird behaviour. The ancient Romans released pigeons and the augus would then interpret messages from the gods from their flight patterns. But all cultures have variations of it. The English owe the old nursery rhyme "One For Sorrow" to it, the counting rhyme that attributes predictive value to the number of magpies you see flying;

> *One for sorrow,*
> *Two for mirth*
> *Three for a funeral,*
> *Four for birth*
> *Five for heaven*
> *Six for hell*
> *Seven for the devil, his own self*

... of which, of course, there are again dozens of variants. Illustrating the many superstitious myths surrounding the magpie. In Western culture, he usually does not come off well. The magpie is considered cunning and thieving, bad luck, associated with witchcraft and said to predict death. And, to add injury to the insult: "A single magpie in spring, foul weather will bring".

The myth that the magpie steals shiny things is actually quite new. Rossini wrote one of his most beloved operas, *La Gazza Ladra* ("The Thieving Magpie", 1817, the opera with Rossini's perhaps most brilliant overture) in 1817, in which a magpie steals a silver spoon. An innocent maid is falsely accused of the theft and sentenced to death. The popularity of opera also popularises this plot, which is then further milked in stories (Lilian Gask's *A Basket Of Flowers*, 1910), in children's books, cartoons and in comics. Culminating in Hergé's graphically stunning, atypical, suspensefully uninspired but humorously irresistible *Tintin and The Castafiore Emerald* (1963) - all comedy-of-errors-like stories that build on the misunderstandings that arise when a magpie steals something of value.

It's not true, by the way. Magpies are exceptionally intelligent birds (the only birds to pass the mirror test, for example), and are mostly curious. They have no particular inclination to steal shiny things. But the myth is persistent, and so we all understand what Martin Carthy means when he characterises Dylan with the words "He was a real magpie".

To the indefatigable, enthusiastic German folklorist Jürgen Kloss and the brilliant work of love on his website *Just Another Tune*, we owe academic confirmation of Carthy's apt observation. Kloss writes the fascinating article "...She Once Was A True Love Of Mine" and in it takes us along on a treasure hunt for the sources for "Girl From The North Country", a scavenger hunt for the origins of all the shiny thingies found by the magpie Dylan.

Kloss acknowledges - of course - and discusses at length the influence of Carthy and "Scarborough Fair", but also analyses that Dylan's song is at best a vague copy of it, or less so, actually: "In fact the differences are so great that it can easily be called an original melody." He then searches and finds a host of sources for the shiny things the magpie gathers. The motif anyway, of the messenger to remind the girl of her former lover, which Dylan already knows from songs like Johnny Cash's "Give My Love To Rose", and the Everly Brothers' hit "Take A Message To Mary". More notable still is Betty Carter's "Tell Him I Said Hello", from which theme and word choice descend both in "Girl From The North Country" and later in "If You See Her, Say Hello";

> *When you see him*
> *Tell him things are slow*
> *There's a reason and he's sure to know*
> *But on second thought, forget it*
> *Just tell him I said hello*
> *If he asks you when I come and go*
> *Say I stay home 'cause I miss him so*
> *But on second thought, forget it*
> *Just tell him I said hello*

Equally widespread is the use of "North Country" as an idealised place of carefree idyll, which Kloss finds in abundance in traditional folk songs, and Dylan's recurring use of it in "North Country Blues", "Ballad For A Friend" and in this song. Or the tender sigh *Please see if she's wearing a coat so warm*, which the German scholar traces to yet other songs in Dylan's baggage, songs like "Baby It's Cold Outside" and Irving Berlin's "I've Got My Love To Keep Me Warm".

Just a few examples of the multitude of shiny things Dylan collects here and there for his song. And just as many arguments to classify the song as an exceptionally successful work in a long, long tradition - rather than as an individual expression of a personal, fundamental formative experience.

Indeed, Kloss also has a commendable aversion to the many biographical interpretations you inevitably come across, to the stubborn, childish attempts of exegetes who try to stick a name from Dylan's environment on the Girl from the North Country. One consensus among all those code-crackers is: Echo Hellstrom, a childhood friend of Dylan's who has the misfortune of being blonde, leading to her having to walk around with the "Muse of

Dylan" stamp for the rest of her life. Longer even; the mere fact that so many fans and Dylanologists want to understand the song as biographical historiography, and that the northern girl then "therefore" is Echo, gives her death news value. Hundreds of newspapers reported on 23 January 2018 that Echo Star Casey, nee Helstrom, "the woman rumoured to be the subject of Bob Dylan's song Girl from the North Country" had died. The song has quite literally become the story of her life; her Wikipedia page describes her life in 761 words, and 697 of them are about Dylan and his song.

It might be a bit sad, such *fame by association*, and all the more so if that association seems to be fictitious and mainly due to sensationalist wishful thinking, but it is what it is. And in the end, for what it's worth, Echo is for millions of people indeed a "shard of glass, an agate bead, a monocle", well alright, maybe even "the emerald", but in any case: at the very least one of the many shiny things with which the magpie Dylan embellishes one of his all-time greatest songs. No small feat, however you look at it.

III   Whatever "country" is

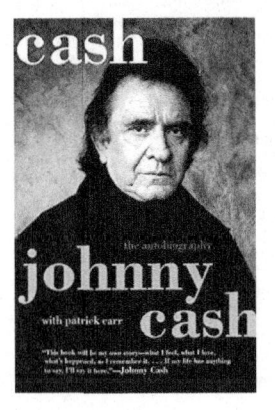

"John R. Cash was an American country singer-songwriter." Thus opens the English Wikipedia page on Johnny Cash, and so do the French, German, Dutch, Russian, Chinese and about 90 more Wikipedia pages: Cash was first and foremost a country artist. The Spanish calls him *el Rey de la Música Country*, the Portuguese *personificação do country*, and actually only the Letzenburgische (Luxembourg)

does not mention a style of music in the first paragraph, but only mentions it at the end of the second paragraph:

> Säi musikalesche Spektrum ass vun den 1950er Jore mat Country, Gospel, Rockabilly, Blues, Folk a Pop bis zum Alternative Country am Ufank vum 21. Joerhonnert gaangen.

... so "country" still does come first. Whereon one could have an opinion, and Johnny Cash himself struggles with it too, in his autobiography. Firstly, with the term itself. "When music people today," Cash philosophises, "performers and fans alike, talk about being 'country,' they don't mean they know or even care about the country and the life it sustains and regulates." The way of life depicted by "country" is long gone, he argues, and what remains are empty symbols of bygone culture. "Are the hats, the boots, the pickup trucks, and the honky-tonking poses all that's left of a disintegrating culture?"

> "The "country" music establishment, including "country" radio and the "Country" Music Association, does after all seem to have decided that whatever "country" is, some of us aren't."

In any case, he himself does not seem to fully understand either why he was pigeonholed as "country musician" from Day One, and that lack of understanding is palpable. His breakthrough hit "I Walk The Line" (1956) may have been a so-called crossover hit, as it reached No 19 on the pop music charts, but it established Cash's name by conquering the combined country charts: six weeks at No 1 on the U.S. Country Juke Box charts, one week at No 1 on the C&W Jockey charts, and No 2 on the C&W Best Seller charts. And when Cash looks around, up there, he sees hits like Elvis' "Heartbreak Hotel" and "Hound Dog", Carl Perkins' "Blue Suede Shoes", Fats Domino's "Blueberry Hill" and Gene Vincent's "Be-Bop-A-Lula", all of which rank collegially alongside Hank Snow, Kitty

Wells, George Jones and Porter Wagoner and all those other country greats... reviewing the *Billboard Top Country & Western Records of 1956*, it is indeed a bit puzzling according to which criteria a song is labelled as "country". At least in the Rock and Roll Hall of Fame, "I Walk The Line" is permanently listed among "The 500 Songs That Shaped Rock and Roll".

He himself tries to arrange a first audition with Sam Phillips as a gospel singer, but that does not convince the legendary Sun Records producer. No market for it, he thinks. Cash then tries as a C&W singer, ironically ("My next try didn't work, either - that time I told him I was a country singer"), is allowed to audition and performs some Hank Snow songs, a Jimmie Rodgers song, a couple of Carter Family songs, but that doesn't please either. Phillips wants to hear a song of his own, so Cash then just plays "Hey Porter" ("Though I didn't think it was any good"). The producer immediately catches on: rockabilly! And with that, Cash has his first record deal: "Come back tomorrow with those guys you've been making the music with, and we'll put that song down, he told me."

The stamp "country" is inescapable, though. And Cash conforms to it. For his second album (*The Fabulous Johnny Cash*, 1958), he writes songs like "Don't Take Your Guns to Town" and "I Still Miss Someone", and records songs by country greats like Bob Nolan and Cindy Walker. But we can already see the love for folk too: the second track is Cash's adaptation of the time-honoured "Frankie And Johnny", in his case "Frankie's Man, Johnny". Which again scores crossover; #9 on the Billboard country chart, 57 on the Hot 100. And he confesses this love of folk wholeheartedly in his autobiography: "I was deeply into folk music in the early 1960s". So he has Dylan in his sights early on:

> "I took note of Bob Dylan as soon as the *Bob Dylan* album came out in early '62 and listened almost constantly to *The Freewheelin' Bob Dylan* in '63. I had a portable record player I'd take along on the road, and I'd put on *Freewheelin'* backstage, then go out and do my show, then listen again as soon as I came off."

With which he appears to be a true connoisseur; at most 2,500 copies of that first album were sold in 1962. So, by his own account, Johnny Cash did belong to that select club of buyers. More fascinating though, and more moving too, is the second part of his declaration of love, about his obsession with *The Freewheelin'*. His words are reminiscent of Lennon's in *The Beatles Anthology* (2000):

> "In Paris in 1964 was the first time I ever heard Dylan at all. Paul got the record [*The Freewheelin' Bob Dylan*] from a French DJ. For three weeks in Paris we didn't stop playing it. We all went potty about Dylan."

And decades later, looking back, both McCartney and Lennon point to its influence. "Norwegian Wood", "I'm A Loser", "You've Got To Hide Your Love Away"... "That's me in my Dylan period again," analyses Lennon in 1980, just before his death. Which Paul agrees, in 1984: "That was John doing a Dylan... heavily influenced by Bob. If you listen, he's singing it like Bob."

Cash - fortunately - does not sing like Dylan, but indeed: from 1962 onwards, when Cash says he is *deeply into folk music*, and so fond of listening to Dylan, we see a turnaround in repertoire choice. On *Blood, Sweat And Tears* (1963), which he recorded from June to August '62, there are songs like "The Legend of John Henry's Hammer" and "Casey Jones", and in 1964 he records the successful *Orange Blossom Special*, with no fewer than three Dylan songs ("It Ain't Me Babe", "Don't Think Twice, It's All Right" and "Mama, You've Been on My Mind").

It makes it all the stranger that Cash makes such a mess of the lyrics of "Girl From The North Country" on *Nashville Skyline*.

If we take him at his word, that he *listened almost constantly to The Freewheelin' Bob Dylan in '63*, before and after every gig on his portable record player, that alone is an impressive number of spins; in 1963, Cash did 61 concerts after the release of *The Freewheelin'* (27 May 1963), so with that fact alone, we count 122 spins of "Girl From The North Country". More than enough to have the lyrics indelibly imprinted on memory, one might say. But it actually goes wrong right from the start.

Alternately, the men apparently agreed. And presumably then the last verse, the repetition of the first verse, together. Dylan, with his new voice, does stay perfectly true-to-text, when he opens. However, when it's Cash's turn after that first verse, he does not sing the second verse, but the third. Sort of, anyway;

Dylan's original	Cash on *Nashville Skyline*
Please see for me if her hair hangs long	*See for me that her hair's hanging down*
If it rolls and flows all down her breast	*It curls and falls all down her* "frest"[?]
Please see for me if her hair hangs long	*See for me that her hair's hanging down*
That's the way I remember her best	*That's the way I remember her best*

... only the last line is unchanged. Which in itself is hardly a problem, of course. Dylan himself is the last person who thinks his lyrics are sacred; "They're songs. They're not written in stone. They're on plastic" (*SongTalk* interview with Paul Zollo, 1991).

Dylan quickly switches gears and then sings the second verse himself, the verse Cash skipped. Ideally, The Man In Black would then do the fourth verse, but alas: he sets in the fifth, the last. Dylan is still alert and quick, and decides in a split second that this will be the last verse then, the two-part duet - Cash has only sung *"If you're..."*, and Dylan is already joining in: *"... travelin', in the North Country fair"*. The second line, *Where the winds hit heavy on the borderline*, then comes out smoothly, but by line three it goes wrong again. Dylan sings, as he should, *Remember me to one who lives there*, but his partner improvises *Please say hello to the one who lives there*. However, Cash has kept his ears open; when the men then sing the same verse one more time, he neatly follows the original lyrics.

Oh well, who cares. It is and remains an exciting combo of two giants showcasing their musical pleasure with a song that is so strong that it cannot be broken anyway. And who knows - perhaps Cash has just sown the first seed for "If You See Her, Say Hello" with his lyrics rehash here. Not an insignificant song either.

IV   A la fille, qui fut mon amour

Dylan's foray into the Great American Songbook, the triptych *Shadows In The Night* (2015), *Fallen Angels* (2016) and *Triplicate* (2017) is special, but not unique; in this category Dylan is, for once, not a trendsetter. As it is, any record shop can fill quite a bin with pop and rock stars venturing into the American Songbook, with quite a few Big Names too. Rod Stewart delivers a whole series (four albums), Bryan Ferry scores as early as 1999 with *As Time Goes By*, Lady Gaga even reaches the No. 1 position with Tony Bennett (*Cheek To*

Cheek, 2014), and repeats that feat a few years later with *Love For Sale* (2021), Annie Lennox, Sir Paul McCartney, Cindy Lauper... one bin is probably not enough in this record shop, in any case.

In 2007, record stores can add the next Big Name: Art Garfunkel's tenth solo album is called *Some Enchanted Evening*, and is, as the title suggests, Artie's take on "I've Grown Accustomed to Her Face", "I Remember You", "Someone To Watch Over Me" and 11 more songs from the Songbook, the songs of Gershwin, Arlen/Koehler, Rodgers/Hammerstein, Burke/Van Heusen and Irving Berlin, the songs that rightly enjoy enduring popularity.

Unfortunately, Garfunkel does not add much. Well, his still crushingly beautiful, angelic voice, obviously - over which there is now a slight, not unpleasant rustle, by the way. Apart from that, though, the record is another staging post in the slow, gradual degeneration of Garfunkel's records, which actually started from the first solo album, 1973's successful *Angel Clare*: with each record, Garfunkel's music becomes more sterile, ethereal and muzak-y. Which, incidentally, is not just down to production; after the second album, the commercially and artistically successful *Breakaway* (1975), Art's instinct for good songs seems to abandon him more and more. *Breakaway* still has only good to exceptional songs: Stevie Wonder's "I Believe (When I Fall In Love It Will Be Forever)", a brilliant version of Antônio Carlos Jobim's "Waters Of March", Paul Simon's gem "My Little Town", Albert Hammond's beauty "99 Miles From L.A." and especially the stratospherical Beach Boys song "Disney Girls" - but after this album, the decline irrevocably sets in.

In both the twentieth and twenty-first centuries, however, Garfunkel is wise enough to let his setlists lean on the Simon &

Garfunkel repertoire. Mainly the more light-headed, ethereal songs like "For Emily, Whenever I May Find Her", "A Poem On The Underground Wall" and "Kathy's Song", but crowd pleasers like "Sounds Of Silence" and "The Boxer" still keep it balanced. And among the ethereal songs, "Scarborough Fair" has now won a permanent place.

Since 2014, "Scarborough Fair" has not been off Art's setlist; from the 1970s until 2013, Garfunkel has performed the song some 30 times, since 2014 it has been performed more than 100 times. To which he then usually adds a remarkable coda: after the final words *parsley, sage, rosemary and thyme*, the song gently flows, accompanied only by a single guitar, into

> *Remember me to one who lives there*
> *She once was a true love of mine*
>
> *If you go when the snowflakes fall*
> *When the rivers freeze and the summer ends*
> *Please see she has a coat so warm*
> *To keep her from the howlin' winds*
>
> *If you're travelin' to Scarborough Fair*
> *When the winds hit heavy on the borderline*
> *Remember me to one who lives there*
> *She once was a true love of mine*

... a music-historically perfect coda, of course, but Dylan's song seems to have fascinated him for some time now anyhow. Back in 1981, Art Garfunkel sings a particularly sterile version of Jimmy Webb's "In Cars" on his understandably flopped album *Scissor's Cut* in which suddenly, again in the coda, we hear Art singing "Girl From The North Country" alienatingly and mixed far, far back, like a ghost in the attic. Too weird and vague to be labelled a cover, but the use of Dylan's song live, in the coda of "Scarborough Fair" that is, makes up for a lot.

Real covers abound, though. Hundreds, if not thousands. Almost all of them beautiful; the song just cannot be broken. At the very least worth mentioning is Rosanne Cash, who, in 2009, began her late father's homework. Johnny Cash once gave Rosanne a list of "100 essential songs", and for her album *The List* she records the first fourteen of them; classics like "Miss The Mississippi And You", "Long Black Veil" and "500 Miles"... and "Girl From The North Country".

Fine, but lacking the intensity of, say, Joe Cocker (with Leon Russell on *Mad Dogs & Englishmen*, 1970), Rod Stewart (who actually always produces great Dylan covers, this one is on 1974's *Smiler*) or - especially - the American guitar beast Walter Trout. The studio version (*Prisoner Of A Dream*, 1991) is superb, but truly goosebump-inducing are the many live versions, in which Trout seems to get into The Zone every time. Not too surprising; in 2017, when Walter against all odds has survived liver cirrhosis thanks to a liver transplant, and has returned to the spotlights, he declares from the stage in Leeuwarden, the Netherlands, that he owes everything to three foundations under his work:

> 1. the release of Bob Dylan's first album,
> 2. The Beatles' performance on 9 February 1964 on the Ed Sullivan Show, and
> 3. listening to Paul Butterfield for the first time.

... by which he no doubt does not mean Dylan's actual *first* album, given his decades-long, unconditional loyalty to the girl from the North, but rather *The Freewheelin'*. "Girl From The North Country" he usually announces as "my favourite song, a song written by my friend Mr. Bob Dylan" - and always he uses the song to demonstrate his exceptional skill with the pinky-swell technique. Usually in the second solo.

Jimmy LaFave, James Last, Ramblin' Jack Elliott, Waylon Jennings, Link Wray, Eels, Eddie Vedder... throw blindfolded a dart into the record shop, and you'll always hit a bin where a cover can be found. Most don't stray too far from the original, staying close in terms of tempo, instrumentation and elegance. Though one might get some extra goosebumps if the song is sung by a real girl from the north, like by the enchanting Ane Brun, with a chilling interpretation on the beautiful album *Leave Me Breathless* (2017).

For the truly special je-ne-sais-quoi, we will have to look not only across national borders, but across language borders. The song can - of course - be found in all languages, and even dialects thereof, and it might be obvious to go first of all to a North Country to find a perfect cover. Plenty of choice there, too. "Flickan från landet i norr", "Hvis du reiser nordover", "Pigen fra det højeste nord"... more than one cover can be found in the national language in every Nordic country. But they, like German, Czech, Hebrew and all the others, have to lose out to the languages that just happen to always sound good: Italian and French.

French wins. There may be plenty *Ragazzi del Nord*, but our Italian friends cannot match the sheer beauty of Francis Cabrel, when he joins forces with Jean-Jacques Goldman (1999), picking up Hugues Aufray's translation, and recording a thoroughly elegant, utterly moving "La Fille du Nord" for the charity project *Sol En Si*.

> *Si tu passe la-bàs vers le Nord*
> *Où les vents souffle sur la frontière*
> *N'oublie pas de donné le bonjour,*
> *À la fille, qui fut mon amour*

A-t-elle encore ses blonds cheveux si long, c'est ainsi que je l'aimais bien... In retrospect, it's a shame Echo lived in Hibbing. And not in Quebec, over the borderline.

12   Wanted Man

I   From Sacramento to Bangor, Maine

> *Wanted man in California, wanted man in Buffalo*
> *Wanted man in Kansas City, wanted man in Ohio*
> *Wanted man in Mississippi, wanted man in old Cheyenne*
> *Wherever you might look tonight, you might see this wanted man*

Dylan's fascination with wanted men, with killers in particular, has been known since the early 60s, and is uncomfortable to this day. The 1975 ode to mafia assassin Joseph "Joey" Gallo is one of the low points in that respect, not to mention the propagandistic nonsense Dylan sings about John Wesley Hardin, the repulsive psychopath who murdered dozens of innocent people for the slightest reason (because they snored, for instance): *"He was never known to hurt an honest man"*, to quote just one blatant lie, and *"But no charge held against him could they prove"* ("John Wesley Harding", 1967).

Whitewashings like "poetic freedom" or "irony" do not make it any less distasteful. Moreover, off-song utterances also give reason to think that Dylan has a peculiar blind spot for the inappropriateness of admiring unscrupulous butchers like Jesse James, John Wesley Hardin and Joe Gallo, and the anecdote told by scriptwriter Rudy Wurlitzer to *Popmatters* journalist Rodger Jacobs in 2009 is illustrative and rather worrying in this regard.

Wurlitzer, incidentally indeed a great-grandson of Rudolph Wurlitzer, the jukebox guy, attracted attention thanks to his script for the cult classic *Two-Lane Blacktop* (1971), the only film to feature James Taylor (in a leading role even, as "The Driver", with a supporting role for Beach Boy Dennis Wilson as "The Mechanic"). The script impresses, is printed in its entirety in the April 1971 issue of *Esquire*, and is noticed by director Peckinpah. "Bloody" Sam then asks Wurlitzer to write the script for his next western, *Pat Garrett And Billy The Kid*, which apparently comes to Dylan's attention.

> "The script was already written when Bob came to see me in my apartment on the Lower East Side of New York. He said that he had always related to Billy the Kid as if he was some kind of reincarnation; it was clear that he was obsessed with the Billy the Kid myth."

Wurlitzer, who at first naturally thinks Dylan is interested in providing the soundtrack, learns to his surprise that Dylan would like to play in the movie. One phone call to producer Gordon Carroll is enough (Carroll, of course, recognises the commercial value of a film poster with Dylan's name on it), and Wurlitzer invents an insignificant supporting role ("Alias") on the spot, and, still back home in New York, quickly writes a few extra scenes into the script.

The rest is history, but Wurlitzer's outpouring about Dylan's obsession with Billy The Kid remains somewhat underexposed - though it really is not that insignificant. It places yet another question mark over Dylan's judgement or, perhaps more painfully, an irrevocable tick in the "rather naïve" box on the list of Dylan's intellectual qualities.

An "obsession with the Billy The Kid myth" and a sense that he is "a kind of reincarnation" of the legendary outlaw suggests that Dylan is confusing romanticised biographies of the desperado with historiography. The dry, factual historiography is quite comprehensive and well-documented, and leaves little doubt about the nature of Henry McCarty alias William H. Bonney alias Billy The Kid; robbing shops from the age of 15, aggressive horse thief, quarrelsome gambler and (at least) eight-time murderer, who needlessly and with apparent pleasure also kills unarmed opponents - there really isn't much admirable or romantic about the actual life story of Billy The Kid. If Dylan feels any kinship at all, it almost certainly has to be with one of Billy's many film incarnations. *The Law vs. Billy the Kid* (1954, starring Scott Brady), for instance, or 1958's *The Left Handed Gun*, with Paul Newman. And songs like Woody Guthrie's version of "Billy The Kid", and otherwise that of Marty Robbins (on one of Dylan's favourite albums, *Gunfighter Ballads and Trail Songs*, 1959), will only have confirmed him in Billy's heroic, ill-fated image;

> *I rode down the border and robbed in Juarez*
> *I drank to the maidens, the happiest of days*
> *My picture is posted from Texas to Maine*
> *And women and riding and robbing's my game*

... subject matter, myth-making and word choice that all lead him to the song he pulls out of his Stetson in a few minutes for Johnny Cash in 1969: "Wanted Man".

The song is not overly ambitious; in fact, no more than a list song over a ten-a-penny chord progression (the time-honoured C-D-G-F-C circle), with an equally unspectacular melody. The trigger for the song doesn't seem too mysterious either. The song is first tried, and presumably written, on 18 February 1969. Six days later, 24 February, Cash is expected in California, at San Quentin State Prison, for the legendary prison concert.

In fact, Dylan's inspiration seems to have been fed far more extensively by Cash's touring schedule than this single, legendary concert at San Quentin. A glance at the Man in Black's tour history does ignite more than one aha-experience:

    24 February - 12 March '69 – California
    12 October '69 – Buffalo
    17 March '68 – Kansas City
    27-28 August '69 – Ohio
    1 December '69 – Mississippi
    14 September '68 – Colorado
    13 August '70 – Georgia
    13 September '68 – El Paso
    21-21 October '69 – Shreveport
    12-13 September '69 – Abilene
    15-18 September '69 – Albuquerque
    14 November '69 - Syracuse

... remarkably many of the place names Dylan lists in "Wanted Man" can be found in Cash's tour schedule. Twelve out of 16 - that's a bit too many to be coincidental. The US has over 19 thousand towns and cities, with Cash performing in 36 of them in 1969, so the chance of Dylan incorporating twelve of them in his song is microscopically small. Thirteen even, if you cheat a bit;

> *Then I went to sleep in Shreveport, woke up in Abilene*
> *Wonderin' why the hell I'm wanted at some town halfway*
> *between*

Exactly halfway between Shreveport and Abilene lies Dallas - where Cash performs on 29 November 1969. Incidentally: still here in Nashville, probably at that same little table, Dylan writes "Champaign, Illinois" as well, for the guitarist on duty during this same session, for Carl Perkins – Cash plays 4 October 1969 in Champaign, Illinois.

All in all, it begins to look very much like Cash's calendar indeed is on the little table at which Dylan quickly writes his song for his friend. Although Take 1, on *The Bootleg Series Vol. 15 1967-1969: Travelin' Thru* (2019) suggests that the song has not literally been completely "written" at that point; Cash has only a basic idea of the lyrics and is just guessing at the place names. "Hibbing" he shouts, for example, gleefully cheeky, and "Duluth". Apparently, he does not yet have a written-out full version of the lyrics. Which are, by the way, very different from the final, official lyrics anyway:

> *Wanted man in Indiana, wanted man in Ohio*
> *Wanted man in Texarkana, wanted man in Mexico*
> *Wanted man in Sacramento, wanted man in old Cheyenne*
> *Wherever you may look tonight, you may see this wanted man*

... with Dylan himself in turn also hopelessly jumbling the lyrics, when repeating this opening couplet - which then turns out to be intended as a chorus:

> *Wanted man in Sacramento, wanted man in Tennessee*
> *Wanted man in Oklahoma, wanted man in... ehmm...*
> ["Muskogee?" Cash guesses]
> *Wanted man in Indiana, wanted man in old Cheyenne*
> *Wherever you might look tonight, you may see this wanted man*

And in the continuation Dylan, clearly à l'improviste, calls out place names like Milwaukee, Minneapolis and Missouri, and an audibly amused Cash does not lag behind. "Bangor, Maine", "Seattle", "Jackson", "Bristol", "Kingston", "Norfolk"... again all place names where he has either performed recently or will perform soon. Yes, by now the conclusion seems inescapable: during this semi-improvised *Take 1*, both men are peeking at the same tour schedule, at Johnny Cash's 1968-69 tour schedule. "Gate City", which Cash playfully calls out at the end, is a charming little town in Virginia (about two thousand inhabitants) where the Man In Black won't play until August 1971, so that's not the trigger; that would be his wife June, also present in the studio – she is from there.

Anyway: in six days, in a California Department of Corrections and Rehabilitation State Prison for Men, Cash will premiere the final version of "Wanted Man".

II   I shot a man in Reno

Wanted man in California, wanted man in Buffalo
Wanted man in Kansas City, wanted man in Ohio
Wanted man in Mississippi, wanted man in old Cheyenne
Wherever you might look tonight, you might see this wanted man

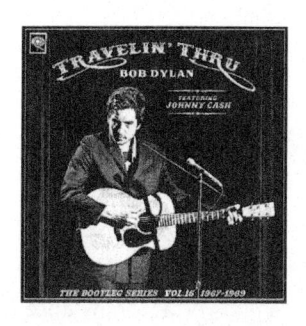

"Last week, uh, in Nashville, Bob Dylan, one of the top writers... well, I don't need to tell you who Bob Dylan is. The greatest writer of our time was at our house, and he and I sat down and wrote a song together. Let me see if I can find that damn thing, I'll sing it for you. Yeah, here it is. It's called Wanted Man. Do you know the introduction Bob? OK." That last question is addressed to lead guitarist Bob Wootton, who then effortlessly splashes a "Folsom Prison Blues"-like intro from his guitar. Which kicks off "Wanted Man" on *Johnny Cash At San Quentin* - the opening track on the legendary album (1969), but number 15 on Cash's actual setlist, that February day in California.

The claim that "he and I sat down and wrote a song together" might be a bit overblown - presumably Cash also noticed that Dylan copied the place names from his tour schedule, or maybe he did spell them out, and therefore feels some kind of authorship. Either way, not a big deal. More interesting are the half-mumbled comment *Let me see if I can find that damn thing*, and the observation that we do indeed see him looking at a paper on his lectern during the song: so by now, six days after that funny Take 1, he has a written-out version of the lyrics. All the more interesting because these - now official - lyrics are so vastly different from the handwritten lyrics published in the 2019 booklet of *The Bootleg Series Vol. 15 1967-1969: Travelin' Thru* (on page 29). *Every* line is different, including the opening couplet/refrain:

> *Wanted man in Carolina, Wanted Man in Buffalo*
> *Wanted Man in Arizona, Wanted Man in Ohio*
> *Wanted Man in Kansas City, Wanted Man in Old Chyanne* [sic]
> *Everywhere you look tonight, boys, I am a Wanted Man*

So far, hardly spectacular differences; "Carolina" instead of "California" or "Kansas City" instead of "Mississippi" is, of course, not that relevant. More fascinating is the rest of that photographed manuscript in the booklet: after this slightly different refrain, we see two-and-a-half more stanzas, including corrections and alternative verses, that differ wholly and utterly from the final text. There is no trace of the first verse, for instance, in the final version:

> *I find a seat in Reno, and I'm doing mighty fine*
> *The boss he tips his hat to me and I in turn tip mine*
> (take my money)
> *I'm just about to collect my winnings, every nickel, every dime*
> (I was born to make this killing)
> *But someone always recognizes me before it's time*

Fine verse, and for Dylanologists, it sheds priceless light on the workings of Dylan's creativity. "*I find a seat in Reno*" and the third alternative of verse 3 "*I was born to make a killing*"... Dylan chooses as his first-person narrator a protagonist who almost automatically imposes himself on him as he sits next to Johnny Cash at a table here:

> *When I was just a baby my mama told me: Son,*
> *Always be a good boy, don't ever play with guns.*
> *But I shot a man in Reno just to watch him die*
> *Now every time I hear that whistle, I hang my head and cry.*

... the leading actor from "Folsom Prison Blues", one of Cash's signature songs, one of his first songs too (written in 1953), and the song with which he scored a No 1 hit just a few months ago, in the summer of 1968 (the live version from *At Folsom Prison*). There is no way Dylan is *not* thinking of the song when he writes the line *I find a seat in Reno*. He himself played "Folsom Prison Blues" with the guys of The Band at the *Basement* not so long ago; in May '69, still in Nashville, he records it during the *Self Portrait* sessions, in 1987 he plays it with the men of The Grateful Dead, and from 1991 onwards it is on the setlist 20 times. When the theme "Jail" is on, at his *Theme Time Radio Hour* (season 1, episode 6), the monument is - of course - the opening song, and DJ Dylan again quotes exactly this line, or rather, he quotes verbatim from *Cash; The Autobiography* from 1997;

> Johnny said he wrote the line *I shot a man in Reno just to watch him die* because he was trying to think of the worst reason for killing another person. He added: "It did come to mind quite easily, though." When Johnny Cash performed first at San Quentin, Merle Haggard was in the audience. And by "audience" I mean: jail.

"Wanted Man" would thus have been set up as a kind of prequel to "Folsom Prison Blues", as the background of the hunted criminal who is eventually, in Cash's song, caught and locked up. Which is a nice idea, and Its execution is also fine - a line like *The boss he tips his hat to me and I in turn tip mine* is already as wonderful a Dylan-worthy line as the opening of this verse, which initially seems to be about a successful gambler. In the second instance, however, apparently *after* Dylan has also written a second and a third stanza, he seems to want to lay the *Folsom Prison* connotation on even thicker, prickling in small print between the third and fourth lines that *I was born to make this killing*-alternative. Nice line, and the hint to "Folsom Prison Blues" is also successful, but: the plot is disrupted. Now it's no longer a successful gambler at a gaming table in Reno, and furthermore the last line, *But someone always recognises me before it's time*, does not fit anymore and should now be rewritten as well.

It is unknown, and somewhat puzzling, why Dylan did not do so. *The greatest writer of our time* should have no problem with that, and the rest of the manuscript demonstrates his "usual" extraordinary form today. He doesn't seem to be short of time either; the handwriting is neat, he uses no abbreviations, no "&" instead of "and", even the past participles are written with end-g (*doing*, *working*), and the manuscript gives four alternate verse lines... time enough, apparently.

No, it almost seems as if a lonesome whistle has suddenly blown away his blues.

III   Now, I admire Merle

> *I might be in Colorado or Georgia by the sea*
> *Working for some man who may not know at all who I might be*
> *If you ever see me comin' and if you know who I am*
> *Don't you breathe it to nobody 'cause you know I'm on the lam*

That first take of 18 February and the song's premiere in San Quentin on 24 February suggest that the manuscript was written before 18 February. Indeed, as Cash reveals at the announcement, at Cash's home. Dylan hears about that upcoming prison concert, may already know that Cash wrote the song "San Quentin" for the occasion, and now offers to contribute a song as well, and Dylan fan Cash gratefully accepts, such a scenario is obvious. Against an alternative genesis, a scenario of Dylan later undertaking a lyric revision, which then is the manuscript we see on page 29 of the booklet, speaks the absence of the best lines from the versions we know, from Take 1 and San Quentin:

> *Then I went to sleep in Shreveport, woke up in Abilene*
> *Wonderin' why the hell I'm wanted at some town halfway between*

... it's not too likely that Dylan would delete these lines when revising "Wanted Man", in any case. No, that manuscript surely is the primal version, rewritten on the spot a day later, in the studio. And we find this *Colorado* couplet broadly reflected in it:

> *I might be in Colorado, or maybe Tennessee*
> *Working for some man who may not know who I might be*
> *But he always gives me notice* [crossed-out word]
> *(But I do not have a number, couldn't get one if I tried*
> *But there's always someone special, whom I must keep satisfied*
> *For I do not have a number, couldn't get one if I tried)*

The first two lines are keepers, but then *the greatest writer of our time* seems to lose his momentum. An unfinished third line, a crossed-out word, and three more variants, all of which - rightly - will not make it: one can virtually *see* the clogging of the creative vein.

The photograph of the manuscript offers three more final lines. Revealing how Dylan is trying to get the engine going again:

> *I eat only when I'm hungry*
> *Now I plot my destination by the lamp inside the can*
> *That is how it is boys when you're a wanted man*

... so, to get started, Dylan once again delves into his inner jukebox. "*I eat only when I'm hungry*" is, of course, the beginning of *I'll eat when I'm hungry and I'll drink when I'm dry* from "The Moonshiner", the old traditional that Dylan has already recorded once at the *Times They Are A-Changin'* sessions in 1963 (a recording eventually released in 1991, on *The Bootleg Series Vol. 1-3*). And it works: he doesn't even have to finish the line, and rushes on to the two closing lines.

"*Now I plot my destination by the lamp inside the can*" is still far from perfect, obviously. On several fronts, even. The choice of words is alienating in a text full of good ol' boys locker room talk, the sentence structure is ramshackle, and a denouement where the Wanted Man is in prison (*in the can*) is not too strong either - in that case, the intended closing line ("*That's how it is boys when you're a wanted man*") is now wrong; after all, when he's in the can, he's no longer a wanted man. But the line presumably does take him to the verse that will make it into the final version: "*Don't you breathe it to nobody 'cause you know I'm on the lam*". At least, that seems obvious because of the homophones *lamp - lam*.

Another, and equally attractive option, is Merle Haggard. The next day, in the studio, Cash seems to give a hint when he jokingly sings/shouts *"Wanted man in Muskogee"*, but that's a coincidence; Haggard's signature song "Okie From Muskagee" is not recorded until a few months later (17 July 1969). Cash played in Muskogee in June 1968 – it's yet again a town from his tour calendar.

In Cash's record cabinet, however, there are undoubtedly plenty of records from his colleague, and surely the two most recent, which happen to be two of Haggard's very best records: *Mama Tried* and *Pride In What I Am*. The latter has just been out for a fortnight and is high on the Country Charts at the time Dylan is staying with Cash. And on *Mama Tried*, the record filled with prison songs like "Green, Green Grass Of Home" and "I Could Have Gone Right", and with the heart-breaking "In the Good Old Days" from the then rather unknown Dolly Parton, also features Merle's cover of "Folsom Prison Blues". Plus the title track, of course, the No. 1 hit that Dylan still admires almost 40 years later, when he jokingly criticises Merle Haggard in his wonderful MusiCares speech (February 2015):

> "Merle Haggard didn't think much of my songs, but Buck Owens did, and Buck even recorded some of my early songs. Now I admire Merle – "Mama Tried," "Tonight The Bottle Let Me Down," "I'm a Lonesome Fugitive." I understand all that but I can't imagine Waylon Jennings singing "The Bottle Let Me Down." I love Merle but he's not Buck."

In the "Post MusiCares Conversation", Bill Flanagan asks just to be sure. Was he really dissing Merle Haggard back there? No, not at all, Dylan says. I have the highest regard for Merle, toured with him, his Jimmie Rodgers tribute album is one of my favourite records, he's a complete man and we're friends these days,

> "I wasn't dissing Merle, not the Merle I know. What I was talking about happened a long time ago, maybe in the late sixties. Merle had that song out called "Fighting Side of Me" and I'd seen an interview with him where he was going on about hippies and Dylan and the counter culture, and it kind of stuck in my mind and hurt, lumping me in with everything he didn't like. But of course times have changed and he's changed too."

And when host Cash puts Merle's new record on the turntable, this February evening '69 in Nashville, Dylan hears in the beautiful opening song "I Take A Lot Of Pride In What I Am" (okay, a rather shameless "Gentle On My Mind" rip-off, but still beautiful):

> *I guess I grew up a loner,*
> *I don't remember ever havin' any folks around.*
> *But I keep thumbin' through the phone books,*
> *And lookin' for my daddy's name in every town.*
> *And I meet lots of friendly people,*
> *That I always end up leavin' on the lam.*
> *Where I've been or where I'm goin'*
> *Didn't take alot of knowin',*
> *But I take alot of pride in what I am.*

... in which he then hears that unusual phrase *"on the lam"* a few times. And the rest of the record will no doubt please Dylan too; the Bakerfield sound, as opposed to the indulgence of Nashville, sprinkled with folk, blues and pop influences, containing wonderful songs like "The Day The Rains Came", Hank Williams-like tearjerkers like "It Meant Goodbye When You Said Hello To Him" and even a Jimmie Rodgers song ("California Blues").

That idle *eat-when-I'm-hungry* line on the manuscript, by the way, keeps buzzing around in the back of Dylan's mind; some

30 years later, in 1997, it finally finds shelter in "Dreamin' Of You" (*Well, I eat when I'm hungry, drink when I'm dry / Live my life on the square*). But tomorrow, in the studio, the men will be singing something else there.

IV To All The Girls I've Loved Before

Wanted man by Lucy Watson, wanted man by Jeannie Brown
Wanted man by Nellie Johnson, wanted man in this next town
But I've had all that I've wanted of a lot of things I had
And a lot more than I needed of some things that turned out bad

In 2015, the Gibraltarian Albert Hammond finally receives the massive bronze statuette of the muse of lyric poetry Euterpe, the award that perhaps should have been given to him several decades earlier: the Ivor Novello Award for his entire oeuvre. Rightly so, but a bit late; by the mid-80s, Hammond already had a respectable number of world hits to his name, either as a performing artist or as a songwriter for others. "It Never Rains in Southern California", "Down By The River", "The Free Electric Band", "I'm A Train", and "When I'm Gone"... all great songs. Not to mention the songs he writes for colleagues. The Hollies' "The Air That I Breathe" is arguably a 70s signature song, Leo Sayer scored his biggest hit with "When I Need You", Art Garfunkel made "99 Miles From L.A." immortal, Grace Slick is thankful for "Nothing's Gonna Stop Us Now", the underrated beauty "Smokey Factory Blues" with which Johnny Cash closes the 1975 *John R. Cash* album (one of his finest records, but The Man In Black doesn't agree in his autobiography: "I wasn't pleased with either the process or the results"), Celine Dion, Whitney Houston, Tina Turner, and we could go on and on; the list is long.

Most of those immortal hits a justifiably proud Hammond performs in the successful concept with which he has toured annually since 2013; the "Songbook Tours". In his crowning year 2015, no fewer than 30 songs are on the setlist, and (usually) on 21 is the world hit that even so few people know was written by Hammond (together with master lyricist Hal David): "To All The Girls I've Loved Before".

True, it *is* a song that indeed comes into its own better when Willie Nelson sings it together with the archetypal womaniser Julio Iglesias: a song of an irresistibly charming bad boy who leaves a trail of broken hearts. We know the archetype from such milestones as The Eagles' "Take It Easy" (*Well, I'm a runnin' down the road, tryin' to loosen my load / I've got seven women on my mind*), The Allman Brothers' "Ramblin' Man", and the 1999 global summer hit, Lou Bega's "Mambo No. 5", the song in which Lou with deep affection sings of the charms of Angela, Pamela, Monica, Erica, Rita, Tina, Sandra, Mary and Jessica.

It has something farcical, of course, and that seems to be the effect Dylan and Cash are aiming for, with this "women's names verse". There is no trace of it yet in the manuscript, and indeed it also seems to be an intervention with the upcoming premiere in mind: Dylan and Cash know that the song will be played in front of a room full of male inmates. And an audience player like Johnny Cash knows he should not only insert an occasional "son of a bitch", a "damned" here and a "what the hell" there, but also that a nudge nudge wink wink to erotic escapades will go down well.

Accordingly, on the concert video, we see Cash singing this verse with a lopsided grin, but cheers from the inmates do not erupt yet - that does not happen until the next verse, which is also absent from the manuscript:

> *I got sidetracked in El Paso, stopped to get myself a map*
> *Went the wrong way into Juarez with Juanita on my lap*
> *Then I went to sleep in Shreveport, woke up in Abilene*
> *Wonderin' why the hell I'm wanted at some town halfway between*

... with "*Juanita on my lap*" in particular seeming to stir up randy fantasies. And apart from that, this seems to be a textual contribution by Cash himself. Or at least initiated by Cash; after all, on 5 October 1965, he was arrested in El Paso while returning from Juarez with 668 Dexedrine and 475 Equanil pills in his guitar case. Thus, "*Got sidetracked in El Paso and went the wrong way in Juarez*" is an admittedly concise but historically accurate summary of that much-discussed misstep. Life imitating art, in other words, to which Jaoquin Phoenix also refers in the crushing biopic *Walk The Line* (2005); Cash has had "Cocaine Blues" on his setlist for years before that arrest in El Paso;

> *Made a good run but I run too slow*
> *They overtook me down in Juarez, Mexico*
>
> *Laid in the hot joints takin' the pill*
> *In walked the sheriff from Jericho Hill*

... not on Dylan's, by the way. Dylan, who has "Cocaine Blues" on the setlist over 70 times between 1961 and 1999, sings the other "Cocaine Blues", the Reverend Gary Davis song, the one with the "*cocaine, running all around my brain*" refrain.

Things end relatively well for Cash. In March '66, the case comes to trial, and The Man In Black shows himself to be a repentant sinner ("I realise my mistake. It was bad, very bad, misconduct on my part"), claims he was tired and drunk, and vows never to take a pill again. Which is a bit odd, as Cash's lawyer argues that the drugs were "prescribed". Which the judge goes along with: because the drugs are "prescribed", *and* perhaps because Tex Ritter and Gene Autry wrote sweet letters to the judge vouching for the "good character" of the accused, Cash gets off with a $1000 fine and a suspended jail sentence. Quite a lighter sentence than Willy Lee from "Cocaine Blues", all things considered;

> *The judge, he smiled as he picked up his pen*
> *99 years in the Folsom pen*
> *99 years underneath that ground*
> *I can't forget the day I shot that bad bitch down*

... which, when Cash sings it at that previous prison concert, in the Folsom Prison cafeteria on 13 January 1968, is also greeted with cheers, applause and laughter. "They were the most enthusiastic audience I have ever played to," Cash later declares.

Dylan never won an Ivor Novello Award, by the way. Others were more worthy each time, apparently. Adam Ant, for instance (*Songwriter of the Year* 1982). And Björn and Benny (*Special International Award*, 2002) and Jon Bon Jovi (2021). But Randy Newman and Jimmy Webb have also already been honoured, so if Dylan hangs on a little longer, he will probably get his turn. Otherwise, he'll just have to make do with his minor prizes, with his Grammy Awards, his Oscar and his Nobel Prize and all those other ones. *I've had all that I've wanted of a lot of things I had.*

V Busted flat in Baton Rouge

Wanted man in Albuquerque, wanted man in Syracuse
Wanted man in Tallahassee, wanted man in Baton Rouge
There's somebody set to grab me anywhere that I might be
And wherever you might look tonight, you might get a glimpse of me

Peckinpah's 1961 film debut, *The Deadly Companions*, was not a great success and would (rightly) have been long forgotten had "Bloody" Sam Peckinpah not become such a big name, later on. The second claim to fame is more impressive. Despite the mediocre acting, clumsy editing and hideous soundtrack, Lowell George apparently endured the movie at least an hour: at two-thirds of the film we hear "Turk" (Chill Wills) say, "We'll be able to burn a fire path through this country *from Tucson to Tucumcari*." Lowell grabs his notepad and has a pillar for the song that will become one of his all-time greatest songs;

And I've been from Tucson to Tucumcari
Tehachapi to Tonopah
Driven every kind of rig that's ever been made
Driven the back roads so I wouldn't get weighed
And if you give me; weed, whites, and wine
And you show me a sign
I'll be willin', to be movin'

Back then, Lowell George is still a member of The Mothers Of Invention, but when Zappa hears the song, he knows he should say farewell and allow Lowell a career of his own. At least, that's the romantic version. Other sources report that Lowell was fired for smoking marijuana. And on *Little Feat Live at the Auditorium Theatre Rochester NY October 18, 1975*, we hear Lowell tell us at the introduction, "I was in a group called The Mothers Of Invention and I got fired because I wrote a song about dope. How about that shit?"

Either way, it's an out-of-category song, which is also recognised by the master; when DJ Dylan plays it in his *Theme Time Radio Hour* in 2008 (ep. 84, "Street Maps"), he appreciatively calls "Willin'" a "crowd pleaser that has grown to become a country classic", and he puts his words where the money is: on stage, where Dylan plays the song ten times. The pleasure with which Dylan sings the opening line of the chorus demonstrates his sensitivity to its magical euphony: *I've been from Tucson to Tucumcari, Tehachapi to Tonopah*. Place names that Lowell George may also have got from Hollywood, by the way; Tonopah is the setting for several episodes of the 60s series *State Trooper*, and in the classic *The Maltese Falcon*, Humphrey Bogart says: "Well, if you get a good break, you'll be out of Tehachapi in twenty years and you can come back to me then." A text adaptation that creates a full circle, coincidentally; in the source text, Dashiell Hammett's book, the archetypal hard-boiled private detective Sam Spade says:

> Spade said tenderly: "You angel! Well, if you get a good break you'll be out of *San Quentin* in twenty years and you can come back to me then."

It means nothing, of course. Lowell chooses the four city locations for their euphony - just as Cash and Dylan throw in two towns *not* on Cash's tour schedule in the last stanza (alright, second-to-last, but the last is a repeat of the first stanza): *Tallahassee* and *Baton Rouge*.

Given its euphoniousness, it is a bit disappointing in how little songs Tallahassee is sung. Presumably, Dylan's record cabinet still contains Bing Crosby's "Tallahassee" (along with the Andrews Sisters, 1947), Nancy Sinatra's "Sugar Town" naturally (*I heard it also rained in Tallahassee*), the rockabilly gem that by now does have a kind of evergreen status, Freddy Cannon's "Tallahassee Lassie" from 1959, and Charlie Daniels' "Cowboy Hat In Dallas". Yet another one of those city name-list songs, by the way, just like Tom Waits' "Had Me A Girl" (*And I had me a girl in Tallahassee*), and also from the early 70s - list songs with place names are popular apparently, in those years.

But "Tallahassee" has been confiscated, forever probably, by Bobbie Gentry, although she doesn't actually sing it at all, of course; *"Today, Billie Joe MacAllister jumped off the Tallahatchie Bridge"* ("Ode To Billie Joe", 1967).

"Baton Rouge" is even less fraught, despite similar euphony. Until 1969, when Cash and Dylan topographically fill "Wanted Man", Louisiana's picturesque capital was actually only mentioned in Chuck Berry's "Back in the U.S.A.";

> *New York, Los Angeles, oh, how I yearned for you*
> *Detroit, Chicago, Chattanooga, Baton Rouge*
> *Let alone just to be at my home back in ol' St. Lou*
> *Did I miss the skyscrapers, did I miss the long freeway?*
> *From the coast of California to the shores of Delaware Bay*
> *You can bet your life I did, till I got back to the U.S.A.*

... and in one of the *Songs That Made Him Famous*, the song Cash and Dylan play half an hour before "Wanted Man Take 1" at this same Columbia Studio A in Nashville, the song Dylan played with the men of The Band at The Basement two years before, and which will continue to appear on his setlist with some regularity well into the twenty-first century: Cash's own "Big River" from 1958;

> *Now, won't you batter down by Baton Rouge, River Queen, roll it on*
> *Take that woman on down to New Orleans, New Orleans*
> *Go on, I've had enough, dump my blues down in the Gulf*
> *She loves you, big river, more than me*

It is a wonderful word combination with an irresistible rhythm and magical sheen of its own, *batter down by Baton Rouge*, and undoubtely it still lingers in the studio air, when the men venture into the first take of "Wanted Man" half an hour later. After all, "All these songs are connected," as Dylan says in his MusiCares speech in February 2015.

Kris Kristofferson hangs out there too, by the way, in Nashville, at Cash House and Columbia Studios. And that eloquent *Baton Rouge* seems to strike a chord with him as well - in these same days, Kristofferson writes his pièce de résistance "Me And Bobby McGee":

> *Busted flat in Baton Rouge*
> *Waitin' for the train*
> *Feelin' nearly faded as my jeans*
> *Bobby thumbed a diesel down*
> *Just before it rained*
> *Rode us all the way to New Orleans*

... "Back In The U.S.A.", "Big River", "Wanted Man", "Me And Bobby McGee"... Baton Rouge does seem to bring out the best, in the greatest songwriters of the 20th century.

VI   There's one place I'm not wanted

> Then slowly, extending from his sleeve,
> A cold, white, satin hand took mine.
> *Hey, I like what you do*, he said to me.
> *I like what you do, too*, I replied. I nearly died.
> Then his hand retracted up his sleeve,
> And Bob Dylan turned and took his leave,
> Disappearing back into the rain.
>
> (Nick Cave, The Sick Bag Song, 2015)

Cave's poetic account of his encounter with Dylan at Glastonbury in 1998 is charming and moving, revealing a sympathetic kinship with Dylan himself: the ability to fully admire the artistry of colleagues. A superlative example of this is demonstrated by Cave in September 2013, when he reflects on the death of Johnny Cash, a day earlier, in *The Guardian*. Already the opening of that personal obituary is touching, thanks to Cave's superior sense of dosed drama:

> "I lost my innocence with Johnny Cash. I used to watch the Johnny Cash Show on television in Wangaratta when I was about 9 or 10 years old. At that stage I had really no idea about rock'n'roll. I watched him and from that point I saw that music could be an evil thing, a beautiful, evil thing."

Cave talks about how Cash continues to fascinate him, that he covers several Cash songs throughout his career (as far back as his Australian punk days, such as "The Singer", which he recorded with his band The Bad Seeds), and what a highlight it is when, in 2000, The Man In Black records his old underground hit, the terrifying "The Mercy Seat" from 1988. In a way, that one cover (on volume 3 of Cash's magisterial American Recordings Series, *American III: Solitary Man*) definitively elevates Cave to the elite. Which he himself seems to realise, as that one cover comes up in almost every interview in the twenty-first century - where Cave always, with due pride, says something along the lines of "it doesn't matter what anyone says, Johnny Cash recorded my song". And in this eulogy in *The Guardian*, he mentions it again himself:

> "He did a version of The Mercy Seat. I got a call from Rick Rubin that Johnny Cash wanted to record it and was that all right. That was pretty exciting. The version is so good. He just claims that song as he does with so many. There's no one who can touch him. I wrote and recorded that when I was fairly young, but he has a wealth of experience which he can bring. He can sing a line and give that line both heaven and hell."

The real highlight, however, is yet to come. In 2002, producer Rick Rubin records Cash's last, and perhaps very best of the American Recordings, *American IV: The Man Comes Around*, when Cave just happens to be in Los Angeles. Rubin calls him and asks if he might want to record a song with Cash tomorrow. Cave has to depart the next day, but he still has a few hours before his plane leaves and is of course keen. He gets to choose a song himself and he chooses the old Hank Williams classic "I'm So Lonesome I Could Cry", the song of which Elvis said "I'd like to sing a song that's probably the saddest song I've ever heard" (*Aloha From Hawaii*, 1973).

> "He arrived, and this man with such extraordinary generosity, such an immense spirit made me feel so much at ease. I suggested this song, and he said: "Hey yeah, Nick, I know that one. Let's do it." And the band started up and we just did it."

The duet is one of the many highlights of that peerless swan song *American IV: The Man Comes Around*.

Dylan's and Cash's public acknowledgement of Cave's talent and the admiration demonstrated, retroactively elevate the already unique cover of "Wanted Man". In 1985, a year before Cave records Cash's "The Singer" (actually: "The Folk Singer") for the superb cover album *Kicking Against the Pricks*, he records "Wanted Man" with his Bad Seeds. Remarkably, by then he apparently has status enough to be allowed to change the lyrics; both Cash and Dylan reportedly gave permission.

Cave injects the song, of course, with suspense and drama. To begin with musically. First a hesitant, searching beginning of a lonely piano chord and a wavering guitar lick over which Cave gloomily sighs *"I'm a wanted man"*, and from 0'17" onwards a crescendo begins with theatrical claps on every beat: it promises to be a classic build-up to a devastating climax. Which just doesn't come: the song keeps building and building and building... but the denouement just doesn't come - capturing perfectly the neurotic, never-ending persecution mania of a wanted man.

Lyrically, there's something going on as well; Cave boldly tinkers with the narrative. In the first three verses, he still remains fairly text proof. The wanted man is wanted in Buffalo and Old Cheyenne, in Albuquerque and Baton Rouge - we recognise the first twelve places from the Cash/Dylan original. Only at the end of the third verse does Cave allow himself a first, insignificant deviation;

> *Wanted man in Arizona, wanted man in Galveston*
> *Wanted man in El Dorado, this wanted man's in great demand*

... three locations coming of his own devising, announcing his first drastic text change:

> *If you ever catch me sleepin'*
> *Just see the price flashin' 'bove my head*
> *Well take a look again my friend*
> *That's a gun pointed at your head*

... the paranoia already suggested by the music is now also expressed more explicitly by the protagonist, compounded by the raw, gasping delivery. Lucy Watson and Nellie Johnson still want him, but now the "Boller Sisters" and "Kid Callahan" also join those bounty hunters, and Cave adds tragedy; I am

> *A wanted man who's lost his will to live*
> *A wanted man who won't lay down*
> *There's a woman kneelin' on my grave*
> *Pushin' daisies in the ground*

... unequivocally adding a deeper layer to the original. The following list of locations where he is wanted are all places with their own historical or discographical connotations: Windy City, Wounded Knee, Death Valley, El Paso, New York City, Laredo and Tupelo, after which the lyrics finally conclude with a tragic, heartbreaking denouement that is not offered by the music:

> *Wanted man in every cat house, wanted man in a many saloons*
> *Wanted man is a ghost in hundred homes, a shadow in a thousand rooms*
> *Wanted man down in St. Louis, wanted man in New Orleans*
> *Wanted man in Mossel Bay, wanted man in Cripple Creek*
> *Wanted man in Detroit City, wanted man in San Anton'*
> *But there's one place I'm not wanted lord*
> *It's the place that I call home*

It is a plottwist with melodramatic overtones, but it brings The Other Man In Black lasting admiration of and acceptance by the two men at the top of Olympus, Johnny Cash and Bob Dylan.

Collateral

I threw it all at the wall

Outtakes they are not, the two songs that, with a bit of good will, we may still throw on the *Nashville Skyline* heap.

"Living The Blues" is recorded on 26 April 1969, also in Nashville, the same musicians, in the same studio with the same producer, more than two weeks after 9 April, the day *Nashville Skyline* hits the shops. Dylan plays the song at his guest appearance on the *Johnny Cash Show*, where he also performs "I Threw It All Away" and, together with Cash, "Girl From The North Country", again with the men who also accompanied him in the studio (Norman Blake, Charlie Daniels, Peter Drake, Bob Wilson, Charlie McCoy and Kenneth Buttrey). Eventually, "Living The Blues" ends up on *Self Portrait*.

"I released one album (a double one) where I just threw everything I could think of at the wall and whatever stuck, released it, and then went back and scooped up everything that didn't stick and released that, too," Dylan writes, rather harshly in his autobiography *Chronicles*, about the songs included on *Self Portrait* (1970). A deliberate attempt at self-sabotage, Dylan explains, to rid himself of the freaks, the idiots, the pushy fans, the guru-seekers and all those others who harass him and his family on a daily basis.

"I had assumed that when critics dismissed my work, the same thing would happen to me, that the public would forget about me."

That disdain is a refrain in his public utterances about the album. "You don't play any songs from *Self Portrait*," says journalist Ben Fong-Torres in January 1974, following Dylan and The Band's second concert in Montreal. "I didn't live with those songs for too long," Dylan answers, "those were just scraped together."

Nor is it any more respectful in 1981, when a journalist at the press conference in Travemünde asks about it;

> "Well that was a joke, that album was put out at a time I didn't like the attention I was getting. I never did want attention. At that time I was getting the wrong kind of attention for things I hadn't done. So we released that album to get people off my back, so they would not like me anymore, that's the reason the album was put out, so people would stop buying my records, and they did [*laughs*]."

... and in 1984, talking to *Rolling Stone* interviewer Kurt Loder, Dylan enriches the story with a motivation, as it will be told in his autobiography as well:

> I said: "Well, fuck it I wish these people would just forget about me. I wanna do something they can't possibly like, they can't relate to. They'll see it and they'll listen and they'll say: "Well let's go on to the next person. He ain't sayin' it no more. He ain't givin' us what we want," you know? They'll go on to somebody else."

So a kind of a joke actually, concludes Loder. But then why a double album? And again Dylan sticks to his self-analysis:

> "Well, it wouldn't have held up as a single album – then it really would've been bad, you know. I mean, if you're gonna put a lot of crap on it, you might as well load it up!"

And definitely official is Dylan's statement from 1985, when Cameron Crowe quotes him in the booklet accompanying the successful compilation box *Biograph*: "I just figured I'd put all this stuff together and put it out, my own bootleg record, so to speak."

A consistent story, then. From the first comment in 1974 to the musings in the otherwise rather unreliable 2004 memoir, thirty years hence, Dylan insists that he considers *Self Portrait*, and by extension "Living The Blues", a pile of rubbish.

But then, this is also the man who can't appreciate *The Basement Tapes* at all, who rejects "Blind Willie McTell", "Red River Shore", "She's Your Lover Now" and dozens of other small and big masterpieces... we don't have to put too much value on Dylan's self-critical ability.

Even more exceptional, finally, is the category of songs that have neither been performed nor recorded by Dylan himself, the category within which "Champagne, Illinois" falls. At least, as far as we know never played or recorded by Dylan himself. But the song's initial inception and subsequent handover to Carl Perkins is believed to have taken place on 1 May 1969, behind the scenes of the *Johnny Cash Show*. Close enough to be allowed to locate the song in the outskirts of *Nashville Skyline*, in any case.

13 Champaign, Illinois

I   You're happy, Tim?

"When you buy a cup of coffee today, do you still know who is responsible for it? Who makes that coffee? The gentleman here, of course, thinks it was Herr Starbuck. But you, Frau Bellini, and I, we both know: This Starbuck can't cook everywhere at the same time. No one knows who made the coffee, the only thing we know for sure is that it wasn't Herr Starbuck."

Er ist wieder da (by Timur Vermes, English title *Look Who's Back*) from 2012 is a phenomenal sales success, despite lukewarm to scathing reviews. Millions of copies sold, a successful film and theatre adaptation, translations in more than 40 languages. The story is set in 2011 and the protagonist is Hitler who has risen from his ashes. The monologue above is an example of the satirical quality of the work; the resurrected Hitler does not yet understand these times, but his criticism, in this case the modern reflex to avoid responsibility, makes sense. And Hitler, who was resurrected only a few days ago, has not even been able yet to learn that "*Herr Starbuck*" also produces television programmes, records and films; Starbucks Entertainment has been around for five years at this point, late summer 2011. And has already scored big hits; Paul McCartney's *Memory Almost Full*, for example, and the film *Akeelah and the Bee* (both in 2006).

Less commercially successful, but artistically partly very successful, is the *Artist's Choice* CD series, compilation CDs filled with the choice of famous greats such as Ray Charles, Yo-Yo Ma and Willie Nelson. Bob Dylan selects his pick for the February 2008 release in the series, and it's a beautiful CD. Eclectic as an episode of *Theme Time Radio Hour*, with lesser-known tracks by Dylan favourites like Wanda Jackson, Junior Wells and Ray Price, a few usual suspects (The Stanley Brothers' "The Fields Have Turned Brown", for example), and also featuring liner notes written by the bard:

> "They're a lot of different ways a record can get under your skin. Sometimes it's the way they sound, sometimes it's the words. Maybe it's a guitar riff or a horn line or maybe you feel like the singer is talking right to you. Some people say it's chemistry but chemistry is too much of a science. A great record is more like alchemy. Here's a bunch of folks who somehow manage to turn lead into gold for a couple of minutes. I hope you enjoy them as much as I do."

And his brief commentaries of the individual songs are just as charming and worth reading. Like the opening track, Pee Wee Crayton's "Do Unto Others" from 1954: "I bet that John Lennon heard this record at a party once and probably didn't even know who did it, but that guitar just stuck in his head" – elegantly referring to the fact that Lennon and Ringo have simply stolen the intro for "Revolution".

The selection of Pee Wee Crayton's "Do Unto Others" seems, in a nutshell, to be a symptom of Dylan's weak-spot for shuffling and rearranging facts, styles, genres and artistic expressions. We know this postmodernist artifice - of course - from his music, which combines centuries of song writing, diverse musical genres and paraphrases from both low and high culture into the oeuvre we all admire. But in other areas, Dylan is just as fond of creating mosaics. The screenplay of *Masked & Anonymous*, his autobiography *Chronicles*, his forging and his paintings - the common denominator of Dylan the literary man, Dylan the visual artist, Dylan the musician and Dylan the scriptwriter is: it's a mixed up, muddled up, shook up world, to quote Ray Davies ("Lola", 1970).

Which also applies to Dylan the DJ.

The listener examining the cover of that Dylan edition of *Artist's Choice* is struck by the name of the "Compilation Producer": Tim Ziegler. A name familiar from episode 66, "Lock and Key", of the *Theme Time Radio Hour*, aired on 30 January 2008, nineteen days before Starbucks releases *Artist's Choice: Bob Dylan (Music That Matters To Him)*.

In this broadcast, the sixth song Dylan plays is "Somebody Done Changed The Lock On My Door" by Wynonie Harris;

> "Back in the forties, you couldn't turn on the radio without hearing Wynonie "Mr. Blues" Harris. Here is one of his recordings for the King record label: "Somebody Done Changed The Lock On My Door".

The DJ makes a small, insignificant mistake. King Records has indeed released plenty of Wynonie Harris' records (the irresistible jump-blues monument *Good Rockin' Blues*, for example, from which Elvis learned "Good Rockin' Tonight"), but precisely "Somebody Done Changed The Lock On My Door" was not released by King Records. And so a phone call is made to the studio by a listening know-it-all, and a dryly comic dialogue unfolds with an increasingly grumpy Dylan:

> TZ: *"Yeah, I've been listening to the show all day, and that song you just played, "Somebody Done Changed The Lock On My Door", well, you know, you told everyone that it was on the King record label and I went to Wikipedia, and sorry to tell you, it was on Apollo Records."*
> BD: "Huh! Whaddayaknow. You're probably right, Tim. You know, sometimes we tell you who wrote the song, what kind of music it is, who else recorded it, but you know sometimes we don't get it right. I mean it's important to remember this isn't a classroom here; this is music we're playing. This is music of the field, the pool hall, the back alley crap game, the barroom and the bedroom. We don't want to make it dusty and academic. It's full of sweat and blood, it's like life itself. If every once in a while we get a name wrong, or we tell you it's on the wrong label, it's not gonna kill anybody, Tim. Just listen to the music."
> TZ: *"Well, I hear what you're saying, but you know... it was on the Apollo record label."*
> BD: "Well, thanks for your call Tim."
> TZ: *"Yeah thanks."*
> BD: "Well, there's just no pleasing some people. That was "Somebody Done Changed The Lock On My Door" by Wynonie Harris. On the *APOLLO* record label. You're happy, Tim?"

Funny. But the Dylan fan's attention has already been caught shortly before, when the caller and the DJ are still exchanging pleasantries:

> BD: Hello caller, you're on the air. What's your name and where you're calling from?
> TZ: *Yeah, my name is Tim Ziegler, calling from Champaign-Urbana, Illinois...*

Not only does *Theme Time Radio Hour* choose the very name of the "Compilation Producer" of the CD that will be released by Starbucks in a few weeks, but Tim Ziegler is also being dragged some 2,000 miles away from his hometown. The real Tim Ziegler has lived and worked on the West Coast all his life (and started his career as a colleague of his current interviewer, as a DJ for KUSF-FM, the University of San Francisco's radio station).

But for some reason, the *mixing up, muddling up, shaking up* DJ moves poor Tim from California to Champaign, Illinois...

II   Oh, how I love you

In most models, the universe was filled with an enormous energy density and enormous temperatures and pressures. Filled with jump blues by men like Wynonie Harris, the songs and stage presence of Chuck Berry and Little Richard, rockabilly, Arthur "That's All Right Mama" Crudup, bluegrass, "Ida Red" and Louis Jordan... the confluence of these leads to a sudden, violent cosmic inflation: the Big Bang of Rock 'n' Roll, Elvis' debut album *Elvis Presley* on 13 March 1956, the first rock 'n' roll million seller. And the ignition of that Big Bang is Carl Perkins, or rather his song, the opening song of *Elvis Presley*: "Blue Suede Shoes", with which Perkins himself had scored his first and only No.1 shortly before.

Not a flash in the pan. After "Blue Suede Shoes" Perkins enriched us with songs such as "Matchbox", "Honey Don't" and "Everybody's Trying to Be My Baby", and Sir Paul McCartney declared the official canonization: "If there were no Carl Perkins, there would be no Beatles".

In short, the music-historical importance of Carl Perkins is difficult to overestimate; the credit Perkins has is infinite. Though he did lose a little of that credit in 1996, two years before his death.

Just like Dylan said about his idol Elvis ("I never met Elvis, because I didn't want to meet Elvis [...] Because it seemed like a sorry thing to do"), you should leave your image of the extra-terrestrial Carl Perkins intact. And not pollute it with too much information.

Go Cat Go! The Life and Times of Carl Perkins, The King of Rockabilly (1996) is a hybrid of autobiography and biography, written by *Rolling Stone* journalist David McGee. A concept that rarely works out well; a self-admiring protagonist and the uncritical admiration of the co-writer, who is almost by definition a fan, is a fatal combination. *Life*, by Keith Richards and James Fox, is a rare exception, and illustrates painfully clearly why the (auto-)biographies of big names like Dr. Ralph Stanley (*Man of Constant Sorrow*, 2010, with Eddie Dean), Judy Collins (*Sweet Judy Blue Eyes*, 2011) or Robbie Robertson (*Testimony*, 2016) are often such toe-curling exercises: unlike many of his colleagues, Keith *does* have self-mockery and the ability to put things into perspective.

The (auto-)biography of Carl Perkins lacks that, self-mockery and sense of perspective. With all its unpleasant consequences: superficial, self-cleansing self-reflection, unreliable anecdotes and embarrassing self-congratulation. Perkins' account of his meeting with Dylan in January 1992 is a case in point. Perkins tells us that he is in New York, at the Plaza Hotel, and that Bob Dylan calls up to his room from the lobby. When Dylan enters his hotel room a few minutes later, Carl barely recognises him. Dylan is "fat", and: "looked like seventy years old with his old beard and matted hair, cap on his head". Perkins' description of the ensuing greeting scene is weirdly alienating:

> "He said, 'Uh-uh. We're brothers.' And he hugged me. And I thought he wasn't gonna turn me loose. His beard was

scratchin' my damn face - I'd just shaved. And he's sayin' in my ear, I love you, man. Oh, how I love you. I love you, Carl.' And had tears in his eyes. 'Let me look at you.' And he just stood there. Said, I'm so thankful. You lived through it."

Dylan also has a present for Carl, "a small gold pin in the shape of a guitar", and hands it over with a seemingly rehearsed, monumentally trite talk:

"There's three thoughts that go with that little guitar," Dylan said. "One is for gettin' well. Two is for gettin' up and gettin' back out. And number three is so the world can keep lovin' Carl Perkins alive."

... which Perkins thinks is deeply moving and he perceives it as "so poetic". He promises to cherish the pin and even take it to his grave (in between they hug again, for the third time now), and Dylan is just as moved: "A man can't ask for more than that," he declares, according to Carl. And with that, Dylan leaves the room and Perkins' life;

"Door shut," Carl recalls. "The little bent-over fat man with the Army coat on and ragged guitar case faded into the streets of New York, and nobody knew who he was."

"Built a little too close to the water," as the Germans so aptly put it in relation to übersentimental, self-affected characters, men who are moved to tears by their own goodness.

It is all so out of character and implausible - it gets almost comical. But then again, we are talking *Carl Perkins*, one of the Very Greats, one of the Patriarchs, an architect, a front man and an eyewitness from the very beginning. So his memories, his opinions and his comments are music historically important, do matter one way or another. And: for the book, co-author David McGee conducted interviews with those involved - including Dylan, in

1994. The reason being, of course, the unique, one-off collaboration between Perkins and Dylan in 1969, the co-production of "Champaign, Illinois", the little ditty that Carl would record shortly afterwards for his nice comeback album *On Top*.

Thanks to McGee's researches, we get a story about the song's genesis. Perkins and Dylan meet during the television taping of a Johnny Cash special, so that must have been May 1, 1969. According to legend, Perkins then visits Dylan in his dressing room, where, again according to Carl, Dylan explains to him that he is not getting anywhere with a new song of his. He is stuck. And he sings out, "over a ragged rockabilly rhythm":

> *I got a woman in Morocco*
> *I got a woman over in Spain*
> *But the girl I love*
> *That stole my heart*
> *She lives up in Champaign*
> *I said Champaign,*
> *Champaign, Illinois*

... a first verse that remains largely unchanged. Only lines 2 and 3 change to *Woman that's done stole my heart*, and the chorus line *I certainly do enjoy Champaign, Illinois* is missing. This seems unlikely, well: half true. Perhaps due to erroneous recall by the then 61-year-old Perkins (this recollection comes from an interview conducted by McGee in 1993). In any case, it is unlikely that Dylan has already added "*Illinois*" without having a rhyme word. But apart from this minor issue, Perkins's account seems credible. Indeed, this is the only part of the lyrics that still has a somewhat dylanesque touch (mainly because of the completely unusual rhyme *Spain / Champaign*, of course). The rest of the lyrics are rather run-of-the-mill, so probably written by a poetically less gifted lyricist like Carl Perkins. Like the second verse:

The first time that I went there
They treated me so fine
Man alive, I'm telling you
I thought the whole darn town was mine

... In which alone the folksy *darn* already suggests that this was not written by Dylan.

Less credible again is Perkins' further staging of the dressing room scene. Allegedly, Dylan plays this first, incomplete verse plus half chorus line, and asks Perkins, apparently unsure, "You think it's any good?" And Perkins, He saw that it was good. He takes over Dylan's guitar and easily dashes off the rest of the song:

> Dylan sat transfixed as Carl worked out a loping rhythm on the bass strings with his thumb, filled in with some quick, stinging runs on the treble strings, and improvised a verse-ending lyric:
> *I certainly do enjoy*
> *Cha-a-am-pai hane, Illinois*
> Dylan said: "Your song. Take it. Finish it."

We weren't there, of course, but: "*transfixed*"? Really? All right, it's a nice song, but no more (well, less, actually). "Transfixed" is, again, very, very out of character. This is May 1969. Dylan already has been seeing quite a bit, this decade. He has worked with master guitarists like Michael Bloomfield and top musicians like Charlie McCoy, he was on stage with Johnny Cash just an hour ago, The Beatles and The Stones are courting him, he is jamming with George Harrison and Eric Clapton, and he has been around the world a few times... With all love and respect to Carl Perkins, Dylan is no longer a rookie who freezes like a rabbit in the headlights when Carl Perkins shakes a few common licks over an ordinary chord progression out of his guitar.

It's hardly "Blue Suede Shoes", after all.

III   So that's where the song is going

I got a woman in Morocco
I got a woman in Spain
But the girl I love that stole my heart
She lives up in Champaign

Still, according to that biography with the great and inevitable title *Go, Cat, Go!* this was all Dylan had written before Carl Perkins took over. It's not much, indeed. The clumsy, tautological third verse line is just filler anyway, and it seems clear that the trigger, or the "catalyst", as Dylan calls it, is just the beauty of the city name "Champaign". "So that's where the song was going all along," the artist says in the 2020 New York Times interview with Douglas Brinkley, about the inspirational power of the three words "I contain multitudes".

The mere word "Champaign" does indeed have a special power. Also, or especially, in the combination, as it is usually used, with sister city Urbana. "Champaign-Urbana" has an ingrained antithesis that is irresistible to any language artist. After all, "Champaign", *campania*, means *plain, field*, while the Latin origin of "Urbana" is *urbanus*: from the city, urban, civilised. Plus, as a free bonus, the association with the homophone *Champagne*, with the festive bubbly drink.

"So that's where the song is going," Dylan the songwriter presumably decides, and will have little trouble finding a rhyme word to get there. "Spain" may not be the strongest rhyme word, but it does almost automatically force a filling of the corresponding verse - the formula *I got a woman in...* surfaces by itself, like the bubbles in a glass of champagne. Dylan, who actually has quite a reputation for disliking repetition, has used the formula himself, not so long ago, in "Outlaw Blues" (*I got a woman in Jackson*), which was already not too original back then either.

In 1927 Furry Lewis already sang *Got a girl in Texas* ("Rock Line Blues"), and a year and a half before Dylan struggled with this "Champaign, Illinois" Ray Pennington scored in the country charts with the song that would become a standard, with "I'm a Ramblin' Man": *Got a girl in Cincinnati*. But under Dylan's skin, there are probably Otis Spann's "Little Boy Blue" (*I've got a girl in Chicago*) and most certainly Hank Snow's "I'm Moving On", the biggest country hit of the 50s;

> *Mister Fireman please woncha listen to me*
> *I got a woman in Tennessee*
> *Keep on moving*
> *Keep a rolling on*
> *You're flying too high*
> *It's all over now*
> *I move on*

An indestructible classic, recorded by The Stones, by Ray Charles, Emmylou Harris and whoever else. Arguably the most beautiful version is done by Johnny Cash, who recorded it again with producer Rick Rubin just before his death, but performed it in the 1980s together with Waylon Jennings, making it sound like a real Waylon Jennings song, with Johnny and Waylon taking the liberty of turning *"I got a woman in Tennessee"* into *"got a pretty mama in Tennessee"*. Dylan played the song with some regularity between 1986 and 1996 (23 times). Mostly as a song on the setlist, and sometimes just at the soundcheck or during rehearsals. Like in February '96, in Phoenix, when he has "I'm Moving On" played after Hank Williams' "(I Heard That) Lonesome Whistle" and before... Carl Perkins' "Matchbox". He seems to detect a connection.

Anyway, the *I got a woman* formula. Dylan seems to want to use it for a list song. A continuous enumeration of places where the narrator has women, who will then be crossed off at the end of each verse against that one woman in the chorus, against that incomparable thief of hearts from Champaign, Illinois. Not very inspired either, of course. Jimmy Martin's "Freeborn Man", for example, with the beautiful, all-encompassing verse

> *I got a gal in Cincinnati*
> *Got a woman in San Antone*
> *I always loved the girl next door*
> *But anyplace is home*

... and thirty years later, on the threshold of the twenty-first century, the formula has lost none of its force, as the phenomenon Lou Bega demonstrates in yet another list-song, but still irresistible mambo, in "I Got A Girl":

> *I got a girl in Paris, I got a girl in Rome*
> *I even got a girl in the Vatican Dome*
> *I got a girl right here, I got a girl right there*
> *And I got a girlfriend everywhere*
> *I got a girl on the Moon, I got a girl on Mars*
> *I even got a girl that likes to dance on the stars*
> *I got a girl right here and one right there*
> *And I got a girlfriend everywhere*

There are hardly any fresh, original interpretations of the formula. Just one, in fact: Josh Ritter's outer category song "Girl In The War" (*The Animal Years*, 2006);

> *Peter said to Paul*
> *"All those words that we wrote*
> *Are just the rules of the game and the rules are the first to go"*
> *But now talkin' to God is Laurel beggin' Hardy for a gun*
> *I gotta girl in the war, man I wonder what it is we done*

... with the coincidental link to Dylan's little ditty in Ritter's final couplet:

> *But I gotta girl in the war, Paul her eyes are like champagne*
> *They sparkle, bubble over, in the morning all you got is rain*

But presumably Dylan is planning a more traditional use of the formula *I gotta woman in*. With as a gimmick something like Jimmy Martin's "Freeborn Man": *exotic women all over the world* versus *the girl next door*, here in Illinois. At least, that is what the first choice "Morocco" suggests. A geographical indication that seems to have an exotic sound for Americans more than for Europeans. Morocco is very close to Europe, but choosing Morocco as location in a film like *Casablanca*, in songs like the first song Graham Nash offers to Crosby and Stills in America ("Marrakesh Express", 1969), as a retreat for poets like Burroughs, Ginsberg and Kerouac, and by Dylan himself in "If You See Her, Say Hello" (*she might be in Tangier*), to name but a few examples, illustrates that "Morocco" is associated by American artists with the excitement of *faraway, strange and exotic*. Especially unfortunate then is the following *I got a woman in Spain*; Spain is only forty kilometres from Morocco, which somewhat dilutes the idea of "I got women all over the world". Plus: unintended of course, but many Europeans will think of the Spanish enclaves in Morocco (Ceuta and Melilla) - with just a little ill will, one might even see these two women as one and the same woman – *I got a woman in Spain, Morocco*.

Not what the poet means, obviously. Though perhaps he did notice the unintentional digression. Anyway, he gets stuck, still manages to squeeze out a weak filler (*But the girl I love that stole my heart*), and finishes it off with the catalyst, with *She lives up in Champaign*. Is that all there is? Yes, Peggy, that's all there is.

Ah, there's Carl Perkins. "Your song," Dylan says. "Take it. Finish it."

14   Living The Blues

All that folknik stuff

No comments are known from Dylan about the uncrowned king of underground comics, Robert Crumb. And comments vice versa are not too flattering: "When Joan Baez and Bob Dylan and all that folknik stuff came out, I just found it irritating. Hated it. It sounded silly to me. Dylan was trying to be "raw" but not convincing." (*Record Collector Magazine*, 15 July 2015).

Nonetheless, it's fairly certain that both icons could have an enjoyable evening together at a table in a juke joint, with enough quarters for the juke box. After all, there is a huge patch of common ground: the deep, deep love of *real, authentic rural music*, as Crumb calls it, the old stuff and *crazy hillbilly Okie singers* and the rugged blues of the 1920s and 1930s, "conjuring up visions of dirt roads and going deep into the back country." Words after Dylan's heart, of course.

Just as close to Dylan's heart is the collection *R. Crumb's Heroes of Blues, Jazz & Country,* 21 songs compiled by Crumb in 2006. Seven songs by *Pioneers Of Country Music* like Dock Boggs ("Sugar Baby") and Hayes Shepherd ("The Peddler And His Wife"), seven *Early Jazz Greats* like Bennie Moten's Kansas City Orchestra and Jerry Roll Morton, and seven *Heroes Of Blues* all idolised by Dylan: the Memphis Jug Band (with "On The Road Again", the song to which Dylan dedicates an essay in his *Philosophy Of Modern Song*), Blind Willie McTell ("Dark Night Blues"), Charley Patton (with "High Water Everywhere") and Skip James's "Hard Time Killin' Floor Blues", among others.

Next to a jukebox filled with Crumb's selection, the men would, in short, undoubtedly forge a deep soul connection. And, who knows, if the tête-à-tête takes place in the twenty-first century, Crumb might even tolerate a single Dylan song in the jukebox. "Dirt Road Blues" perhaps, or "Crossing The Rubicon", one of those songs harking back to older blues. Although for the versatile bandleader of the Cheap Suit Serenaders, that is also presumably still too inauthentic; even recognised greats like Howlin' Wolf and Muddy Waters are to him "electric stuff, wanting to be seen as sophisticated, to embrace the prevailing urbanity." And anyway, he is not a fan of jukeboxes either, for that matter: "By 1939 there were 400,000 jukeboxes! That immediately eliminates so many live musicians - a juke joint, which is where jukeboxes got their name from - would fire the barrelhouse pianist."

No, for all the sympathy Fritz the Cat's father will feel for the intentions of, say, "High Water (For Charley Patton)" or "Red River Shore", he will dismiss those masterpieces too for being "sophisticated", as inauthentic. Not to mention the songs Dylan himself dares to call "blues". "Just Like Tom Thumb's Blues", "Outlaw Blues", "Subterranean Homesick Blues", "Tombstone Blues"... fan favourites, but also songs that *embrace the prevailing urbanity*. On which, by the way, Dylan himself may also have a more nuanced opinion in his later years;

> "To me, the blues are a more rural, agrarian type of thing. And even when they're taken to the big city, they still remain that way only pumped up with electricity. That's the thing: I mean, we're listening to all this music today, it's all electricity. Electric guitars, electric bass, electric synthesizers – it's all electronic. You don't really feel somebody breathing, you don't feel their heart in it. The further away you get into that, the less you're going to be connected to the blues. The blues to me is just a pure form, like old country music."
> *(London Press Conference, 4 October 1997)*

Crumb will nod in agreement. And then somewhat sardonically inquire how Dylan would then categorise his own "Living The Blues".

"Irony," Dylan might reply. After all, there is a certain incongruity between words like

> *Since you've been gone*
> *I've been walking around*
> *With my head bowed down to my shoes*
> *I've been living the blues*
> *Ev'ry night without you*

... and the neatly coiffed, blue-eyed, conservatively dressed good family man singing these words soothingly, standing in the glamorous setting of *The Johnny Cash Show*.

In fact, exactly what he had an opinion about seven years ago, in the liner notes of *The Freewheelin'*:

> "What's depressing today is that many young singers are trying to get inside the blues, forgetting that those older singers used them to get outside their troubles."

Still, it *is* a charming song. But miles away from what both the elder Dylan and Robert Crumb associate with "blues". That, of course, already applies to the song's template, the time-honoured "Singing The Blues", which also really should have been called "Singing A Schlager", and, like Dylan's dilution, is mostly sophisticated, polished and artificial – up to a point, authenticity really does co-determine the art pleasure.

Crumb sets the example both in the selection of his compilation album and in images; the bonus to Crumb's wonderful tribute *R. Crumb's Heroes of Blues, Jazz & Country* is a collection of drawn portraits of the heroes, colourful *trading cards,* like baseball cards, with the heads of Son House, Blind Willie Johnson, Leroy Carr and all those others, everyone drawn with the love and respect of a devout fan. But the most love and beauty Crumb puts into the graphically stunning comics that tell the life stories of his blues heroes in black and white, compiled in *R. Crumb Draws the Blues*. Also containing one of Crumb's absolute masterpieces, "Patton", the life story of Charley Patton, which oppressively and overwhelmingly depicts what *living the blues* really is like - from the struggle to follow your calling, the violent and fatal love adventures, the pub fights, the madness, the flood catastrophe, the wandering on the deserted dirt roads to the death that slowly creeps into first

Patton's life and then his songs and finally, three days before his 43rd birthday, fells him. Patton's fatal lover Bertha Lee sits at his deathbed, otherwise his passing goes unnoticed.

With Dylan's lyrics, then, Crumb will have some peace. At least, there is little offence in it for a man who longs for "that sound of something old and atavistic" - after all, "Living The Blues" is entirely free of sophistication; three unimaginative, clichéd couplets with easy-going rhymes like *I don't have to go far / To know where you are* and a bridge with all the poetic depth of, say, Roscoe Holcomb's white hillbilly music, of Crumb's beloved "authentic rural music". Still, as far as the rest goes... No, though Crumb, generally speaking, is particularly modest and reticent about his own music recordings, in this case he had probably stood up, stopped "Living The Blues", and put on something from his own Cheap Suit Serenaders. "Crying My Blues Away" (*Chasin' Rainbows*, 1993) presumably;

> *I sit around and twiddle my thumbs*
> *make not a sound and nobody comes*
> *with my head hanging low*
> *I'm crying my blues away.*

And it is quite likely that the Dylan of the twenty-first century would then have slid a quarter across the table. "Play it again, Robert."

It didn't go nowhere

> "The songs reflect more of the inner me than the songs of the past. They're more to my base than, say *John Wesley Harding*. There I felt everyone expected me to be a poet so that's what I tried to be. But the smallest line in this new album means more to me than some of the songs on any of the previous albums I've made."

Dylan does not shy away from big words, in the interview with Hubert Saal for *Newsweek*, a week before *Nashville Skyline* is released. But they don't last. Less than a decade later, in the *Rolling Stone* interview with Jonathan Cott, autumn 1978, Dylan analyses:

> "Anyway, on *Nashville Skyline* you had to read between the lines. I was trying to grasp something that would lead me on to where I thought I should be, and it didn't go nowhere – it just went down, down, down. I couldn't be anybody but myself, and at that point I didn't know it or want to know it."

... so, much less consistent than his opinion of *Self Portrait* over the years. With regard to *Nashville Skyline*, Dylan's judgement within the span of a decade shifts from *the smallest line means more to me than some of the songs on any of the previous albums* to *you had to read between the lines* and the somewhat puzzling observation that "it didn't go nowhere", and that it "just went down". And concluded with words he also used 12 years earlier, in an interview with Robert Shelton looking back on the first, unsuccessful, sessions for *Blonde On Blonde* in New York, i.e. before the much-discussed, influential move to Nashville:

> "Oh, I was really down. I mean, in ten recording sessions, man, we didn't get one song ... It was the band. But you see, I didn't know that. I didn't want to think that."

Producer Bob Johnston is credited with the brilliant solution of transplanting Dylan to Nashville. Partly out of opportunism, presumably - Nashville is his hometown, after all - but also because he has seen what magic can happen; a few months ago, Supreme Nashville Cat Charlie McCoy, visiting New York, effortlessly played in the guitar part for "Desolation Row" in one single take. And thus hurled into the stratosphere the song for which Dylan, after endless, increasingly desperate attempts, just couldn't find the *je-ne-sais-quoi*.

That was August 1965. A few months later, when Dylan becomes desperate again in unsatisfactory attempts to get the songs for *Blonde On Blonde* on tape, Johnston does not have to insist for long when he suggests to go and seek happiness in Nashville, with Charlie McCoy and his Nashville Cats.

It is a happy, fruitful marriage. *Blonde On Blonde* is followed by the understated masterpiece *John Wesley Harding*. Again recorded at Nashville's Columbia Studios, again with producer Bob Johnston, and featuring a superior selection of Nashville Cats (Charlie McCoy and drummer Kenny Buttrey, plus steel guitarist Pete Drake on two songs). And the once again surprising *Nashville Skyline* then closes the Nashville trilogy.

It's a matter of definition, but nevertheless, it's a bit of an exaggeration to see *Nashville Skyline* as the starting shot, or a founding father of country rock - which is still trumpeted especially in Dylan circles. Long before Dylan's album, the preliminary skirmishes had been delivered by genre-transcending crowd favourites like The Beatles ("Act Naturally", "I've Just Seen A Face"), The Rolling Stones ("High And Dry"), Buffalo Springfield and Ricky Nelson. And Gram Parsons fans do have a point when they point to the album *Safe At Home* (recorded in 1967) by Gram Parson's International Submarine Band as the Big Bang of country rock - and otherwise surely Gram's subsequent project, his joining The Byrds and the resulting milestone *Sweetheart Of The Rodeo* (1968) does qualify.

Either way, Dylan at the very least made Nashville and country rock highly respectable. And Dylan's bleak analysis *it didn't go nowhere* is kind of true; despite a slight reappraisal in the twenty-first century, its follow-up *Self Portrait* is and remains disappointing, and the early years of the 1970s are the years of total creative emptiness - the years when Dylan sits watching the river flow by, waiting for the inspiration to paint a masterpiece.

"All those terms are so over-used, especially 'country music,' that I don't know what it is today. In my mind, it has one or two meanings."

- interview with Nick Krewen, *Long Island Voice,* September 11-17, 1997

Sources

> *Well, I investigated all the books in the library*
> *Ninety percent of 'em gotta be burned away*

Dylan:

- *Writings & Drawings* (1973)
- *Lyrics 1962 - 2001* (2004)
- *Lyrics 1961 - 2012* (2016)
- www.bobdylan.com
- *Tarantula,* 1971
- *Chronicles* (2004)
- *The Freewheelin' Bob Dylan* (1963)
- *Bringing It All Back Home* (1965)
- *Nashville Skyline* (1969)
- *The Bootleg Series 15 - Travelin' Thru, 1967-1969* (2019)
- *Theme Time Radio Hour* (2006-08)
- *MusiCares speech* (2015)
- *The Philosophy Of Modern Song* (2022)

Interview fragments (in addition to the titles mentioned):

- *Every Mind Polluting Word* (collected interviews, compiled by Artur Jarosinski, 2006)

On Dylan (in addition to the titles mentioned):

- *Why Dylan Matters* – Richard F. Thomas, 2017
- *Revolution in the Air* - Clinton Heylin, 2009

- *No Direction Home* - Robert Shelton, 1986
- *Down The Highway* - Howard Sounes, 2001
- *The Double Life of Bob Dylan, Volume 1: A Restless, Hungry Feeling, 1941-1966* - Clinton Heylin (2021)
- *Liner notes Biograph* - Cameron Crowe, 1985
- *Dylan & de Beats* – Tom Willems, 2018
- bjorner.com
- bobdylaninnederland.blogspot.nl
- Untold Dylan (https://bob-dylan.org.uk/)
- expectingrain.com

Miscellaneous (in addition to the titles mentioned):

- *Fortunate Son* – John Fogerty, 2015
- *The Sick Bag Song* – Nick Cave, 2015
- *Wild Tales, A Rock & Roll Life* – Graham Nash, 2013
- *First Time Ever: A Memoir* – Peggy Seeger, 2017
- *This Wheel's On Fire,* Levon Helm, 1993
- *Testimony,* Robbie Robertson, 2016
- *Der Vater eines Mörders* – Alfred Andersch, 1980
- *The Dreamer* – Cliff Richard, 2020
- *Life* – Keith Richards/James Fox, 2020
- *Bluegrass: A History* - Neil V. Rosenberg, 1985
- *Tellin' Stories* - Tim Burgess, 2012
- *High Fidelity* – Nick Hornby, 1995
- *31 Songs* – Nick Hornby, 2002
- *Cash: The Autobiography* – Johnny Cash, 1997
- *Er ist wieder da* – Timur Vermes, 2012
- *Go Cat Go! The Life and Times of Carl Perkins, The King of Rockabilly* – Carl Perkins/David McGee, 1996
- *R. Crumb Draws the Blues* – Robert Crumb, 1992

Notes

Between 2018 and 2023, most of these chapters were published as articles on the British site *Untold Dylan*.

Thanks

Tom Willems, from *bobdylaninnederland.blogspot.nl* - the mercury Dylan blog, author of *Dylan & The Beats,* 2018

Martin Bierens - dear old Bobhead, from Utrecht to Amsterdam to Dornbirn to Stadskanaal to Tilburg to Bielefeld

Tony Attwood - webmaster of *Untold Dylan,* the place where it's always safe and warm

Larry Fyffe, the Knight with the Red Pencil in New Brunswick

Stephen Vallely, double-checking Eagle Eye from Middlesborough

The author

Bob Dylan's songs continue to fascinate.

Jochen Markhorst (1964) grew up in Arnhem, The Netherlands and in Hanover, Germany, with *Highway 61 Revisited* and *Blonde On Blonde* as soundtrack, bought *Blood On The Tracks* and *Street Legal* from his pocket money, studied German language at Utrecht University, translated Russian at the Military Intelligence Service, teaches language training courses at companies and lessons in schools, translates German literature, Dutch websites and English subtitles and always plays the music of Dylan in the background.

Markhorst, however, is not one of the hardliners who honour the motto *Nobody Sings Dylan Like Dylan* – Jimi Hendrix is certainly not the only one who can brush up a Dylan song. He preaches this controversial opinion, among other things, in his fourteen books on Dylan songs, and continues to build on the Dylan library.

Jochen has been living in Utrecht for the past 40 years, is still married to the same great, attractive woman and has two sons who have left home by now, but fortunately still work and live in Utrecht.

In the same series:

Printed in Great Britain
by Amazon